WALKING IN
SHERWOOD FOREST AND
THE DUKERIES

HERITAGE TRAILS IN
SHERWOOD FOREST AND THE DUKERIES

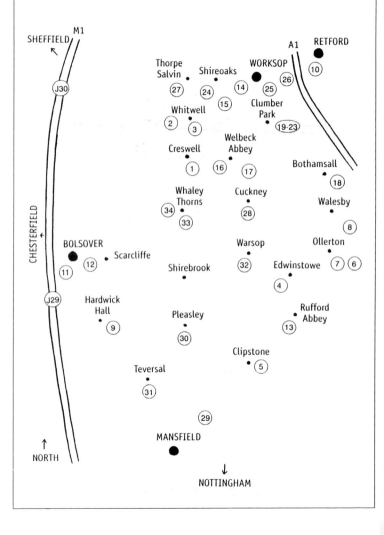

WALKING IN SHERWOOD FOREST AND THE DUKERIES

by
Elaine Burkinshaw

CICERONE PRESS
MILNTHORPE, CUMBRIA

© E. Burkinshaw 1999
ISBN 1 85284 279 2
A catalogue record for this book is available from the British Library.

ADVICE TO READERS

Readers are advised that whilst every effort is taken by the author to ensure the accuracy of this guidebook, changes can occur which may affect the contents. It is advisable to check locally on transport, accommodation, shops etc. but even rights-of-way can be altered and, more especially overseas, paths can be eradicated by landslip, forest fires or changes of ownership.

The publisher would welcome notes of any such changes

Front cover: A view of The Chapel of St Mary the Virgin
from Clumber Bridge

CONTENTS

Introduction

WHERE ARE SHERWOOD FOREST AND THE DUKERIES?

Sherwood Forest and the Dukeries is a compact region situated in the heart of England in North Nottinghamshire. The ancient Royal Hunting Forest of Sherwood once stretched 20 miles from Worksop in the north down to Nottingham in the south and was up to 8 miles wide. The ex-coalfields and a number of distinctive limestone gorges on the Nottinghamshire / North East Derbyshire border run along the western side and the Trent Valley sits over to the east. The Dukeries lie at the northern end of the original forest, with Worksop being regarded as 'The Gateway to the Dukeries'.

WHAT ARE THE OBJECTIVES OF THIS WALKING GUIDE?

Much of the landscape is a rural, gently undulating mixture of blocks of woodland and plantations, farms, parks, lakes and waterways. It is also an area steeped in history and legend with an astonishing variety of historical sites, including a number of major tourist attractions and a tapestry of pretty villages and market towns all in close proximity. Even the extensive ex-coalmining industry, which until fairly recently had such an important impact on the economic development as well as the appearance of the area, now blends unobtrusively into the scenery. Indeed, large areas of 'new countryside' are being created by the regeneration of old colliery sites and opencast mining areas.

With easy access from the M1 and A1, North Nottinghamshire is a growing tourist magnet, encouraged by the initiatives of various bodies to open up public access to the countryside, in the form of country parks, visitor centres, long distance footpaths and the likes of the Center Parcs leisure complex near Edwinstowe. The region may not have the spectacular or dramatic scenery of, for instance, the neighbouring Peak District, but it is distinctive and aesthetically pleasing. However, its recreational potential is still very much undervalued by the visitor and I would like to think that this guide will help to raise the profile of the area.

From the point of view of either the local enthusiast or the visitor, the hidden delights create enchanting and interesting rambling country. A combination of the natural beauty of the countryside, an abundance of wildlife, along with the romantic rich broad based archaeological, architectural and industrial heritage of the region, produces a selection of leisurely and tranquil walks. The routes are based on a network of generally well maintained and defined paths on meandering terrain. The links with Robin Hood provide both an extra dimension and a unique place in the nation's folklore.

My research has revealed that a variety of regeneration projects has taken place in this area in recent years and that there are numerous other exciting initiatives currently being worked upon or in the pipeline. The partnership approach between the various local community projects is paying dividends, though to increase the general level of sustainable tourism will require careful co-ordination and sophisticated marketing of what the area has to offer as a whole.

A HISTORICAL OVERVIEW OF SHERWOOD FOREST AND THE DUKERIES

The Norman Conquerors were keen hunters and creators of the royal forests and the restrictive forest laws. Indeed, it is these detested laws that are the most likely origin of the Robin Hood legend, as any person who dared to defy them, known as an outlaw, would certainly have been regarded as a hero of his day.

Sherwood remained popular with successive medieval monarchs for hunting. However, from the sixteenth century onwards the ownership of the forest began to change. The Tudor and Stuart monarchs were less obsessed with hunting and the forest laws gradually lapsed. With the dissolution of the monasteries much of the land was sold to aristocratic families, who over the next few centuries built large imposing mansions set in landscaped parklands. During the eighteenth century five of these estates at the northern end of the forest had Ducal owners and hence the term Dukeries came into existence.

Worksop Manor is the most northerly estate and once belonged to the **Dukes of Norfolk**. In its time this was arguably the most grandiose house in the area. What is left of it is now a private property.

Clumber Park was created for the **Dukes of Newcastle**, but today it is owned by the National Trust and offers 3800 acres of beautiful parkland to the public.

Welbeck Abbey has remained in the private ownership of the family of the **Dukes of Portland** and access to the estate is strictly limited to marked public footpaths.

Thoresby Hall at the southern end of the Dukeries was once the domain of the **Duke of Kingston**, but it is now privately owned.

The estates at **Haughton** and **Kiveton**, which were respectively owned by the **Dukes of Newcastle** and **Leeds**, no longer exist. Rufford Abbey is usually considered part of the Dukeries, although none of its owners ever achieved the rank of a duke.

The story of the various dukes is a little complicated at times and this is exacerbated by dukedoms becoming extinct, because there was no male heir. This, however, did not prevent the dukedom being recreated at a later stage. As an example, there were three creations of the Dukes of Newcastle Upon Tyne. Thus, over the passage of time there was the 1st Duke of the first creation, the 1st Duke of the second creation and the 1st Duke of the third creation. Also, there were many marriages between certain wealthy families and Christian names were often repeated and passed down to future generations

The creation of the ducal estates slowed the decline of the forest, but in other areas trees were felled to meet the demands of the navy and iron industries and farming. The appearance of the first coalmines, along with the construction of the railways, then led to further destruction of the forest. Two world wars also took a great toll on the forest, although in between the wars the Forestry Commission came into existence and it began re-planting conifers. Since 1945 there have been dramatic improvements with much of the remaining tracts of the forest now in the hands of various conservation organisations.

Sherwood has an international reputation and is, of course, associated with the adventures of the legendary outlaw and popular hero of the common people, Robin Hood and his merrymen. It is fascinating that in this modern age of hightech super-heroes the tales of Robin Hood live on so strongly and remain the principal tourist magnet to the area. However, it must not be overlooked that the forest is also famed for its natural history.

BESS OF HARDWICK AND THE EARLS OF SHREWSBURY

Many of the links between the walks in this book can be traced back to Bess of Hardwick, as the families of the Dukeries were all directly descended from her or were connected by marriage. Bess was said to be the richest and most powerful woman in England after Elizabeth I and is celebrated for building an elaborate and innovative mansion known as Hardwick Hall.

Indeed, her fourth and last husband was the 6th Earl of Shrewsbury, who is likewise a famous historical figure best known for his guardianship of Mary Queen of Scots. The family history of the Talbots, who became the Earls of Shrewsbury and were powerful landowners, is an interesting story in its own right, but is unfortunately well beyond the scope of this book. The 1st Earl was Sir John Talbot, a notorious captain of the One Hundred Years War.

THE SMYTHSON ARCHITECTURAL DYNASTY

Throughout this book you will also find reference to a less well known family, who over three generations had a profound effect upon the development of architecture in Tudor and Stuart England, particularly in the East Midlands. The Smythsons brought freshness and originality in their designs amounting to a Renaissance in English architecture. Instead of medieval fortified buildings their symmetrical prodigy mansions were magnificent, compact and practical.

Robert Smythson's early work can be seen at Longleat House in Wiltshire and Wollaton Hall near Nottingham. John Smythson followed in his father's footsteps, and in turn his son Huntingdon Smythson also became a renowned designer. All three generations were probably involved in Bolsover Castle and their other local contributions include Hardwick Hall, Worksop Manor lodge, Thorpe Salvin Hall, Barlborough Hall and Shireoaks Hall.

HOW TO USE THIS WALKING GUIDE

The structure of this book is simple and yet at the same time it is a little unusual. All the walks are based on a theme and whilst they may obviously be completed in any particular order a certain amount of logic has been applied to relate some of the highlights of the history of the region in a journey through time. To produce a series of walks accompanied by a chronological history is not a particularly revolutionary concept, but it is not the norm as far as walking books are concerned.

Whilst many of the walks fall within the boundaries of North Nottinghamshire and the generally accepted definition of Sherwood Forest and the Dukeries, a number of trails have also been included on the North East Derbyshire and South Yorkshire border where it is felt to be appropriate and in keeping with the themes of the book.

All the routes are circular, ranging from 5 kilometres (3 miles) to 14.5 kilometres (9 miles) and have been designed to be completed in a relaxing half day. Each walk is preceded by a comprehensive local history guide capturing the atmosphere of the scene and providing a flavour of the historical treasures you will see along the way to complement your enjoyment of the walk. Hopefully, you will have the time and feel inspired to explore the attractions in more detail, or perhaps you may choose to return at a later date, as the historical sites visited are an integral part of the local heritage.

In researching the historical content of this book it soon became apparent that compared to many other areas of England this part of Nottinghamshire appears to have been neglected in terms of the structured historical information that is on sale to the public. Indeed, books specifically relating to the history of Nottinghamshire concentrate heavily towards the southern end of the county around Nottingham itself. Why the detail available is so sparse is a little unclear, but is likely to be due to a combination of factors, including the difficulties in following the family history of the various dukes and the fact that all the remaining properties are not open to the public.

However, bearing in mind that this book is primarily a walking guide, a short history narrating the focal points has been compiled from an extensive range of sources. Specific emphasis has been placed upon identifying various links between different trails with Bess of Hardwick and her descendants providing the main vehicle for many of these relationships. The book utilises a tremendous variety of attractions such as:

- The site of some of the earliest human remains found in Britain at Creswell Crags

- Sections of the Creswell Archaeological Way - a 13 mile trail from the Meden Valley to Whitwell

- The most extensive area of ancient oakland in Europe (Sherwood Forest) and the most famous tree in Britain (the Major Oak)

- Sections of the Robin Hood Way - a 100 mile plus long distance footpath linking many of the sites associated with the tales and exploits of Nottinghamshire's most famous son

- Numerous Elizabethan and Tudor mansions, including those in which the prolific Smythson architectural dynasty played a part

- Designated country parks and visitor centres, some of which were once coalfields

- The Chesterfield Canal - the canal towpath, known as the Cuckoo Way, is a gem not to be missed, providing miles of delightful easy walking country from Chesterfield to the River Trent at West Stockwith

- The River Poulter, River Meden and River Maun, which run in this order from north to south across the region and have in the past provided power for the mills situated next to them

- The Pleasley Trails Network - a series of recreational trails (Teversal, Rowthorne and Meden), which were created from disused railway lines. This framework of the industrial past now acts as an important corridor for wildlife

- The setting of D.H. Lawrence's controversial novel *Lady Chatterley's Lover*

- Pilgrim Fathers movement

- The last open field crop rotation system in England at Laxton

The basic route instructions then follow. A sketch map of the route is also included purely for illustration. For navigational purposes it is recommended that you use the Ordnance Survey, Explorer 28 Sherwood Forest map which covers many of the walks in this book on a suitable scale of 4 centimetres to 1 kilometre. Alternatively, the appropriate Ordnance Survey Pathfinder map provides detail on the same scale.

Wherever possible, the walks in this book follow legal public rights of way. Rights of way are the single most important means by which we can enjoy the countryside and preserve it for future generations. Briefly, these comprise public footpaths (foot only), bridleways (on foot, horseback and pedal cycles) and byways (usually old roads used as public footpaths, for example, green lanes). If you find your right of way obstructed, you should report the details to the appropriate County Council. Walkers usually have free access to canal towpaths and country parks and also to land owned, for instance, by the Forestry Commission or the National Trust. However, if you are in any doubt please always check with the owner. On occasions permissive or concessionary footpaths have been used. These paths are shown on maps but there is no legal right to use them and, therefore, they may be extinguished at any time.

Please respect ancient sites and remember to observe the Countryside Code:

- Guard against all fires
- Fasten all gates
- Keep dogs under proper control
- Keep to paths across farmland
- Avoid damaging fences, hedges and walls
- Leave no litter
- Safeguard water supplies
- Protect wildlife, wild plants and trees
- Go carefully on country roads
- Respect the life of the country

Early Man

TRAIL 1: Creswell Crags

Distance:	7.25 kilometres/4.5 miles
Start:	Creswell Crags visitor centre
Maps:	OS Sherwood Forest Explorer 28
	OS Pathfinder 762 (SK47/57) Staveley & Worksop
	(South)
Refreshments:	Limited selection at visitor centre
Toilets:	Visitor centre
Key features:	Creswell Crags and visitor centre, a section of the
	Robin Hood Way and the Portland family's private
	church at Holbeck

Creswell Crags is a dramatic limestone gorge honeycombed with caves, which bisects the Nottinghamshire / North East Derbyshire border. Following the discovery of human remains in the late

Creswell Crags pond

nineteenth century this minature Cheddar Gorge has become a site of historic and archaeological interest of international importance. It has been designated a Site of Special Scientific Interest for both its geology and natural history. Some of the earliest remains of man in Britain dating back to 40,000 BC and Neanderthal Man have been discovered at Creswell, along with numerous artefacts of human and animal remains through the Ice Age around 13,000 BC and a later distinctive culture which has been named Creswellian Man.

The Cragsd - Creswell was once part of the Welbeck estate and the Duke of Portland had the pond created as a duck shooting lake.

The Caves are all barred to prevent public access. The main caves are:

- Boat House Cave - the Duke kept his boat for the lake in this cave
- Robin Hood's Cave - the alleged inhabitant needs no further explanation
- Mother Grundy's Parlour - named after a nineteenth century witch who apparently lived in the cave
- Pin Hole Cave - in the last century it was custom for each visitor to leave a pin in the rock pool near the entrance
- Church Hole Cave - this cave has provided some of the finest specimens from the Crags

Creswell Crags Visitor Centre is a joint council venture providing an interpretation and appreciation of the importance of the narrow ravine in the evolution of man through interactive exhibits.

Holbeck is a small estate village close to the main entrance to Welbeck. It has a tiny private church with impressive graves of the Portland family.

ROUTE INSTRUCTIONS

1.   From the visitor centre car park, which is on the route of the Robin Hood Way, walk past the visitor centre and take the path immediately off to the left, signposted "To The Crags". Walk past the sewage works on your left up to the Crags Pond.

2.   There is a path down each side of the pond and either option may be taken.

3.   At the end of the pond turn left and head up to a stile. Climb the stile and continue uphill for 20 metres to a waymark post. Here,

TRAIL 1: Creswell Crags

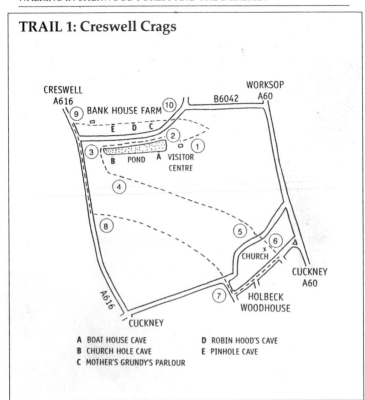

A BOAT HOUSE CAVE
B CHURCH HOLE CAVE
C MOTHER'S GRUNDY'S PARLOUR
D ROBIN HOOD'S CAVE
E PINHOLE CAVE

turn sharp left and on reaching the brow of the hill look for a stile in the far left-hand corner of the field.

4.   Climb the stile and follow the wall edge, which later becomes a wire fence, on your left. The clear path then begins to swing right to a stile. Climb the stile and follow the waymarked path straight ahead across several fields until you reach the road in Holbeck.

5.   Turn left, and then immediately right at a signpost onto a surfaced tree-lined track. Halfway down this track, on the right-hand side, is the Portland family's private church (St Winifred's).

6.   On meeting a road, leave the Robin Hood Way by turning

Creswell Crags

right. Walk through Holbeck Woodhouse and where the road forks, take the right-hand fork. At a T-junction turn right and walk to another T-junction.

7.   Cross the road and follow the signposted track in front of you, which is hedged on both sides. This clear track takes you to the A616.

8.   At the road turn right and follow the footpath along the right-hand side of the A616 into Creswell. Shortly after crossing a road junction off to the right, which leads to the Crags, turn right at a signpost and head up towards Bank House Farm.

9.   Follow the track around the right-hand perimeter of the farm, which shortly becomes hedged on both sides.

10.   On reaching the B6042 turn left. After 50 metres turn right at a signpost. Follow the path along the left-hand edge of the field. At the end of the hedge the path turns right and meets a track. Turn right onto the track and go through a gate, which leads back to the car park.

TRAIL 2: Whitwell and the Markland Grips

Distance:	9.75 kilometres/6 miles
Start:	Car park next to Whitwell Health Centre on Station Road
Maps:	OS Sherwood Forest Explorer 28
	OS Pathfinder 762 (SK47/57) Staveley & Worksop (South)
Refreshments:	Public houses in Whitwell
Toilets:	None
Key features:	The Markland Grips, Burnhill Grips, Whitwell and a section of the Creswell Archaeological Way

The Markland Grips - Grips is a local term used in respect of a steep sided gorge. The Markland Grips consist of two separate limestone gorges (Markland and Hollin Hill) and, whilst smaller, they are arguably more picturesque than their much more famous neighbour at Creswell. Dr Armstrong started excavations in the area in 1924. Evidence of early man and animal occupation, including a Neolithic burial site and an Iron Age fort, have been uncovered.

The area was once a popular picnic spot. The addition of a viaduct, built by the Lancashire, Derbyshire and East Coast Railway Company in the late nineteenth century, led to the district being known as Little Monsal Dale (Monsal Dale is a tourist attraction in the Peak District).

Burnhill Grips was another favourite picnic site of a bygone era. Ashtree Cave was discovered here in 1938 by Dr Armstrong and evidence of the woolly rhinoceros and other animal artefacts came to light.

Whitwell is a village in North East Derbyshire with a rich history and an attractive mix of old and more modern buildings. This walk passes a number of properties of particular interest including:

- **Bakestone Moor Old Post Office** on Sandy Lane
- **St Lawrence Church** - a very fine example of a twelfth century Norman church with fourteenth and fifteenth century additions located on High Street. Inside is the tomb of Sir Roger Manners (son of Sir John Manners and Dorothy Vernon of Haddon Hall in the Peak District)
- **Whitwell Hall** - In 1592 the Old Hall was purchased by Sir John Manners, the son of the Earl of Rutland, from Elizabeth Hardwycke, a distant relation of Bess of Hardwick. The Manners family, as the Dukes of Rutland, continued to live at the hall until 1813 when the Duke of Portland purchased it

  The hall has now been carefully restored and is a private dwelling, reached by turning left after St Lawrence Church onto Old Hall Lane. The hall is on the left-hand side. From an architectural point of view the hall is of great interest as it has an unusual floor plan and whilst the property is not open to the public, if you have a special interest in this type of premises the owners will by appointment provide a tour. The Victoria & Albert Museum in London has a painting of the hall called *Whitwell Hall, Church and Crags* dated 1785 by Samuel Grimm.

- **Manor House** on High Street is one of the oldest buildings in the village
- **The Old George Inn**, now flats, on High Street was once an eighteenth century coaching inn built on the Chesterfield to

Worksop turnpike road
* **Lilac Cottage** across from the George Inn was probably used as the inn's stables
* **The Old Blacksmith's Shop** on High Street has a wheelwright's stone built into the garden wall

ROUTE INSTRUCTIONS

1.   From the car park turn right onto Station Road and then left at the junction onto Portland Street passing Whitwell Community Centre on your right. Portland Street soon becomes Titchfield Street as you head uphill. When you reach Southfield Cottage on your left, the road then becomes Bakestone Moor. Follow the road as it bends to the right and continue until you reach the crossroads, where a left turn takes you onto Sandy Lane. *The Old Post Office is on the corner.*

2.   The tarmac lane soon becomes a rough track. At a crossroad of tracks continue ahead up a short steep hill and follow the clear zigzag path as it drops down at the other side. The path now keeps

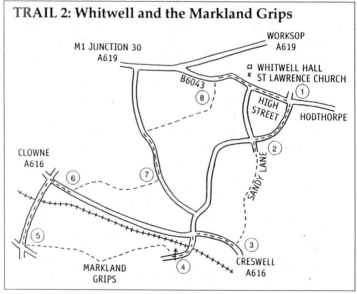

TRAIL 2: Whitwell and the Markland Grips

to the left-hand side of a hump, before climbing over it. *The hump was the 538 yard Whitwell tunnel built in 1874 by the Midland Railway Company for the Mansfield to Worksop line.* At a T-junction of tracks turn left. The tunnel is now on your left. At a fork, head to the right and climb a stile. The track leads downhill past Lower Mill Farm to the A616.

3.   Cross the road and turn right to walk on the pavement past the North Derbyshire Tertiary College. Turn left onto Hazelmere Road. Lower Mill is on your right. Follow the road for 350 metres and turn right at a public footpath sign to join the Creswell Archaeological Way.

4.   Climb the stile and follow the tarmac track. At the end of the farm buildings of Upper Mill Farm watch out for a small waymarker post off to the left. The path initially is walled on the left, but soon becomes a wire fence as you continue along the valley bottom of the gorge. Climb a stile and at a fork keep to the higher path off to the left. Cross another stile and then head under an old railway tunnel to your left. At the end of the tunnel turn right and keep on the main path until you reach a wide track, which is a disused railway track. Turn left, and after 100 metres turn left again at a small waymarker sign onto a track hedged on both sides. At the end of the track, climb over a stile into a field. Walk across the middle of the field with Markland Farm on your left to a water trough in a large gap in the hedge. In the next field make for the far left-hand corner and climb the stile onto the road.

5.   Turn right and then immediately right again at the T-junction. Follow the road, passing Clowne Linear Park on your left, until you reach a crossroads. Turn right onto the A616 for 100 metres and then climb a stile in a wall on your left.

6.   The path heads up to the far right-hand corner of the field and then turns right onto a track. Continue to a wall end and turn left. After 10 metres turn right over a stile. The path heads across a field to the corner of a wood and then continues along the edge of the wood on your right to a lane.

7.   Turn left and follow the lane to the brow of a hill. *The limestone outcrop of Burnhill Grips can be seen on your left as you walk up the hill.* Turn right onto a waymarked track and head downhill. At a T-junction of tracks turn left to leave the Creswell Archaeological

Way. The track emerges onto the B6043.

8.   Turn right and walk into Whitwell on High Street. *St Lawrence Church is on your left.* At the bottom of High Street cross back over to Station Road and return to the car park.

TRAIL 3: Whitwell and Steetley Chapel

Distance:	9.75 kilometres/6 miles
Start:	Car park next to Whitwell Health Centre on Station Road
Maps:	OS Sherwood Forest Explorer 28
	OS Pathfinder 762 (SK47/57) Staveley & Worksop (South)
Refreshments:	Public houses in Whitwell
Toilets:	None
Key features:	Whitwell Wood, Steetley chapel and the Shireoak

ROUTE INSTRUCTIONS

1.   From the car park turn right onto Station Road and right at the junction heading uphill. Take the first left onto Hangar Hill and turn right at a T-junction onto Doles Lane. After 20 metres turn left at a public footpath sign and follow the clear winding track across fields to the A619.

2.   Cross over and join a rough track called Firbeck Lane, which eventually becomes a surfaced road. *On your left is Whitwell Wood, which is owned by Welbeck Estates and is managed by the Forestry Commission. Set on clay soils evidence of early man has been found in this ancient broadleaved woodland, which supports an abundance of interesting flora and fauna. A number of waymarked walks have been laid out in the wood. When you reach the surfaced track the infant shireoak can be seen to the right. The original shireoak marked the point where the counties of Yorkshire, Derbyshire and Nottinghamshire merged.* At a crossroad of lanes continue ahead and then turn right at a T-junction. As the lane bends to the left turn right at a signpost onto a track.

3.   At a crossroad of paths turn right and follow the edge of Scratta Wood, which is on your right. *This is another site where excavations have uncovered Iron Age and Stone Age settlements.* On reaching Dumb

Hall Lane turn right. *Just before a T-junction the small secluded Norman architectural gem of Steetley chapel can be seen on the right. Built in 1120 the chapel is regarded as having a high architectural value in particular for its doorway. Prior to its restoration in 1880 by J. Pearson it had become derelict and had been used for cockfighting and as a sheepfold.* Turn right at the T-junction.

4.   On reaching the A619 cross over and continue ahead up the driveway to Burnt Leys Farm. The route heads past the farm and becomes a rough track close to some large gates. After 150 metres the trail bends to the right. When the track ends continue ahead on a path across the middle of a field.

5.   Turn left onto Doles Lane and eventually retrace your steps back to the car park.

TRAIL 3: Whitwell and Steetley Chapel

The Ancient Royal Hunting Forest of Sherwood

TRAIL 4: Robin Hood Country

Distance:	12.75 kilometres/8 miles
Start:	Sherwood Forest visitor centre off the B6034 in between Edwinstowe and the A616
Maps:	OS Sherwood Forest Explorer 28
	OS Pathfinder 780 (SK66/76) Ollerton
	OS Pathfinder 779 (SK46/56) Mansfield (North) & part of Sherwood Forest
Refreshments:	The visitor centre and public houses in Edwinstowe
Toilets:	The visitor centre
Key features:	Sherwood Forest visitor centre, the Major Oak and a section of the Robin Hood Way

Sherwood Forest is one of the most famous forests in the world. Sherwood means "shire wood", the wood of the shire of Nottingham. It was once one of the largest of the ninety or so royal forests, which were at their most prolific in the thirteenth century, covering much of England.

One of the remaining tracts of this former royal playground set in the heart of the old forest has been designated Sherwood Forest Country Park. It is managed by Nottinghamshire Council and incorporates a visitor centre, which houses an exhibition about Sherwood Forest and Robin Hood. It also acts as a tourist information centre. The park comprises 450 acres of ancient gnarled oaks, shimmering silver birch glades or "birklands" and heath. The "stag headed" oaks are particularly evocative as they are fashioned into grotesque and incredibly weird shapes.

It is important not to overlook the fact that Sherwood is as famed for its natural history as it is for its connections with Robin Hood. Much of this area is a Site of Special Scientific Interest, due to the abundance of old trees and the rare insects that the habitat is able to support. Some of the old 'rides' created by the Dukes of Portland (see Welbeck Abbey), who made this part of the forest their own private pleasure ground for riding and carriage driving, can still be seen.

The Major Oak is a famous large old oak tree set near the Sherwood Forest visitor centre. It weighs an estimated 23 tons, has a trunk of 10 metres and a 28 metre canopy. The tree is approximately 800 years old and it now has to be propped up and fenced off, as the compounding of the soil around it by the sheer volume of visitors was preventing water from reaching the roots. According to legend Robin Hood hid in this tree from his enemies. Originally, the tree was known as the "Cockpen", but after a local historian called Major Hayman Rooke published a book on the oaks of Sherwood Forest in 1790, it became known as "The Major's Oak".

Robin Hood - Sherwood Forest is, of course, inseparably linked with the name of Robin Hood and his companions. The true identity of the elusive outlaw has never been established despite extensive research over many centuries. However, his legend lives on and Sherwood Forest is seen by many as the traditional setting. Indeed, the area reeks the atmosphere of the tales of the daring exploits of this "man of the people", who championed justice and symbolises good and evil.

Popular folklore has depicted Robin historically at the time of the Crusades during the reigns of Richard the Lionheart and his brother John. Others claim that Robin's time was during the reign of Edward II. There have been ballads, plays, stories and more recently a string of films, including Kevin Costner's *Prince of Thieves*, which have continued to capture the imagination of the public and perpetuate the legend. In addition, it is probably fair to say that the lack of historical fact in the search for Robin Hood has contributed to the fascination with this enigma. The power of the myths and legends of Robin are very much on a par with those associated with the magical King Arthur.

Many local places have been associated with Robin Hood including:

- The Major Oak - see above
- Edwinstowe church - see below
- Blidworth - Will Scarlet is alleged to have been laid to rest here

- Papplewick - Alan-a-Dale married a maiden here rescued by Robin Hood from a knight

Edwinstowe is an ancient royal village named after Edwin, the seventh century King of Northumbria, 'Stowe' meaning the burial place. Penda, King of Mercia, killed Edwin at the Battle of Hatfield in 632. After his death he was made a saint in recognition of his efforts as a Christian to vanquish the heathens. According to legend, Edwin was buried in the forest near the village and a chapel was built over the spot.

Edwinstowe church is said to be where Robin Hood wed Maid Marian. The Church of St Mary is mentioned in the Domesday Book, although the present church dates back to 1175. Inside the church is the 'Sherwood Forest Measure', the 'foot' used for measuring forest land, which is 1.5 feet long.

Archway House, also known as the Duke's Folly, was built by the Duke of Portland at Welbeck in 1842. It copies the Gatehouse to Worksop Priory and has statues, which include Robin Hood and his men. The archway was part of the Duke's ride from Welbeck to Nottingham. The house is now a slightly odd looking private residence.

ROUTE INSTRUCTIONS

1.   From the car park follow the signs to the visitor centre. At the entrance to the visitor centre turn left and walk as instructed to the Major Oak on the Robin Hood Way. On reaching the Major Oak, the first left is signposted to Edwinstowe; your route takes the second left.

2.   At a crossroad of paths, turn right to temporarily leave the Robin Hood Way onto a public bridleway. Keep on the bridleway and continue ahead where it crosses a public footpath. At a T-junction turn left and then immediately right at a crossroad of tracks entering the Dukeries Training Area.

3.   This track rejoins the Robin Hood Way. Keep ahead on the clear track with the woodland on your left and an open area on your right. Ignore all side turns until you reach a crossroad of public bridleways and turn left. The track drops downhill to another signposted crossroads. Turn left onto a public footpath called

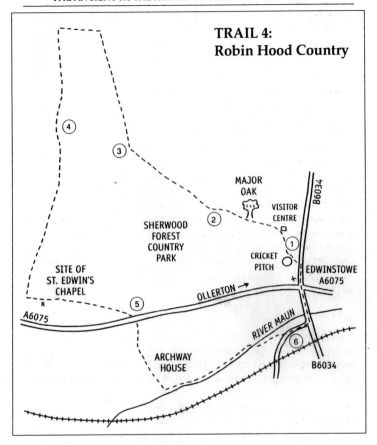

TRAIL 4:
Robin Hood Country

Hanger Hill Drive, which is a surfaced track. *The woodland in this area once belonged to the Dukes of Portland, who used it for recreational purposes and one of the old 'rides' can clearly be seen.*

4. At a junction of tracks turn right following the Robin Hood Way. When the track bends sharply to the right and downhill, continue straight ahead on a path. At a yellow fire hydrant turn left. *One hundred and fifty metres after a crossroads a cross erected by the Duke*

of Portland in 1912 on your right-hand side by the hedge marks the site of St Edwin's Chapel (King Edwin of Northumbria). Keep to the track that runs alongside fields on your right until you reach the A6075.

5.   Cross the road onto the track opposite, which bends to the right. The track passes Archway House on your left and drops down to the River Maun. At a public footpath sign just before the bridge turn left and follow the riverside path. At a public footpath sign turn right and proceed over two footbridges close together. The path continues along the other side of the river to a road in Edwinstowe. By the time you reach the road you will have left the Robin Hood Way.

6.   Turn left and walk to a T-junction with the B6034. Turn left and go over the river. When the road bends to the left, continue straight ahead at the No Entry sign for motor vehicles. At the crossroads with the A6075 continue ahead passing Edwinstowe church on your left. On reaching the cricket ground on your left, take the path around the right-hand side of the pitch. At a fork, turn right to leave the cricket ground and shortly afterwards turn right again at a crossroads. This path leads back to the visitor centre.

TRAIL 5: King John's Palace

Distance:	9.75 kilometres/6 miles
Start:	Vicar Water car park off the B6030 at New Clipstone
Maps:	OS Sherwood Forest Explorer 28
	OS Pathfinder 779 (SK46/56) Mansfield (North) & part of Sherwood Forest
	OS Pathfinder 780 (SK66/76) Ollerton
Refreshments:	Public house in Old Clipstone
Toilets:	None
Key features:	Remains of King John's Palace at Old Clipstone

Sherwood Forest attracted royal visits over several centuries. Often the visitors would stay at **King John's Palace** at Clipstone, which was built in the middle of the twelfth century by Henry II and was named after one of his sons. In its day the palace was a grand hunting lodge providing a convenient place to stay in the middle of the forest, rather than travelling from Nottingham Castle all the

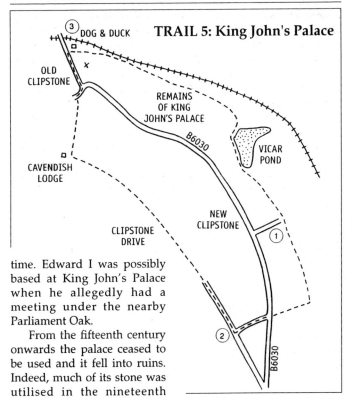

TRAIL 5: King John's Palace

time. Edward I was possibly based at King John's Palace when he allegedly had a meeting under the nearby Parliament Oak.

From the fifteenth century onwards the palace ceased to be used and it fell into ruins. Indeed, much of its stone was utilised in the nineteenth century for local irrigation schemes. Today little is left to see, but the stark ruins do provide a very atmospheric setting.

ROUTE INSTRUCTIONS

1.   From the car park turn right in front of a pond to join a clear track. Turn right at a signpost next to the Bridleways Guest House and Holiday Homes. Cross over the B6030 and continue in the same direction along Newlands Drive. Keep ahead at the next junction and then turn right at a T-junction onto Clipstone Drive.

2.   Clipstone Drive soon becomes a rough track with houses on

your right and later fields. Ignore all side turnings, eventually reaching Cavendish Lodge. In front of the lodge the track bends to the right and becomes a surfaced lane. Turn right on reaching a T-junction and then left at another T-junction in 30 metres. The road passes through Old Clipstone.

3.   Enter the car park of the Dog and Duck public house on your right by a signpost. Walk diagonally across the car park to join a rough track, which later becomes surfaced at various stages. *If you look over to your right from the public house the ruins of King John's Palace come into view.* Continue ahead at Haskell & Co and pass under two bridges before reaching Vicar Pond. Turn right on reaching the pond and follow the lane around the edge of the pond and then through a long tunnel. At a junction turn right and return to the car park.

Country Villages and their Traditions

TRAIL 6: Laxton - Open Field Crop Rotation System

Distance: 5 kilometres/3 miles
Start: Laxton visitor centre car park next to the Dovecote Inn
Maps: OS Pathfinder 780 (SK66/76) Ollerton
Refreshments: Dovecote Inn - Laxton
Toilets: Visitor centre
Key features: Laxton visitor centre, a tour of Laxton village and the Mill Field

Formerly part of the Thorseby estate, Laxton has remained largely unchanged since Norman times. It is a fascinating and unique off the beaten track village, which is famed as the only village in England to preserve the traditions of the medieval open field system of agriculture. Laxton represents not just a step back in rural history, but also a social way of life.

In the Middle Ages there were four open fields around Laxton, but today only three remain unenclosed. **Mill Field** is the oldest and largest. West Field and South Field are the other two. Every year one is left fallow in the crop rotation process. Each field is divided into narrow strips. The unploughed land, called sykes, acts as pasture and also provides drainage.

The administration of the system is in the hands of the Field Jury, who are responsible to the Court Leet. The latter meets annually at the Dovecote Inn in the village.

Initially, **Laxton** appears to be like any other village. However, the older buildings, which are mainly eighteenth century, are farmhouses built side on to the main street with small paddocks behind them. In times of 'communal' farming the village community was usually situated in the middle of the fields. The eighteenth century enclosure movement, on the other hand, drew farmers to

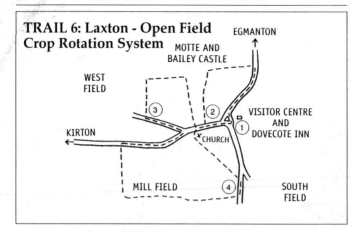

build their home on their own land away from the village.

Laxton is also well known for its fine motte and bailey castle, which dates back to shortly after the Norman Conquest. However, by 1300 the castle was already in ruins as it ceased to be of any military importance.

A visitor centre has been set up in the outbuildings of the Dovecote Inn, depicting aspects of this obsolete system of husbandry. There are public footpaths providing easy access to view all three fields.

ROUTE INSTRUCTIONS

1.   Turn right out of the car park onto Bar Road passing Bar Farm and New Bar Farm. One hundred and fifty metres after a left-hand bend turn left onto a signed public bridleway. The path crosses two fields and then bends to the left and heads towards the church.

2.   At the road turn right and in 50 metres turn right again onto a track by an information board about the Church of St Michael. After 100 metres by a gate you will find another information board about the motte and bailey castle ahead of you. Turn left onto a path hedged on both sides. Cross a stile and then turn immediately left

Steetley Chapel (Trail 3)

Creswell Crags (Trail1)
The Major Oak, Sherwood Forest Country Park

to cross another stile. Follow the field edge with a hedge on your right to a lane.

3.   Turn left and then right at a T-junction. Leave the road at a signpost for Mill Field. At the second crossroad of tracks at an information board for Mill Field turn left. At first you are in open country, but the path heads gently downhill to be hedged on both sides until you reach a lane.

4.   Turn left and after 100 metres, opposite Manor Farm, turn left over a stile by a signpost. Turn right to follow the field edge as it bends to the left. Look out for a yellow waymarker on a telegraph pole at which point the path bears to the right to a gate and footbridge. Head uphill towards the far left-hand corner of the field. There is a stile just to the right of a tennis court. Cross the stile and walk to the left-hand side of the church to a gate. Pass through the gate and the graveyard to a road. Turn right and return to the Dovecote Inn.

TRAIL 7: Wellow - Maypole

Distance:	8 kilometres/5 miles
Start:	Wellow Dam
Maps:	OS Sherwood Forest Explorer 28
	OS Pathfinder 780 (SK66/76) Ollerton
Refreshments:	Public houses in Wellow
Toilets:	None
Key features:	Wellow Dam, the earthworks of Jordan Castle and Wellow village

Wellow is a small village close to the medieval open field village of Laxton. Like Laxton, Wellow is still practising its strong countryside traditions, as it is one of only three villages in the country to still have a permanent maypole.

The centrepiece of the village is the lovely green, which is surrounded by seventeenth and eighteenth century pretty cottages, two public houses and the twelfth century parish church of St Swithen. Much of the church was restored in 1878.

On the green is a 60 foot maypole. The present maypole is made

33

The maypole at Wellow

of steel and was erected in 1976, although earlier versions were made of timber from Sherwood Forest. Towards the end of May each year the May Festival takes place and a new May Queen is crowned, celebrating both the onset of summer and the restoration of Charles II.

Wellow was featured in the children's book *The Secret World of Polly Flint*, which was written by Helen Cresswell and later became a television series.

To the north-east of the village the earthworks of **Jordan Castle** can be seen. Richard Foliot and his son Jordan fortified Jordan Castle in 1264.

ROUTE INSTRUCTIONS

1.   From the car park next to Wellow Dam take the track down the right-hand side of the dam. This clear path leads into and follows the edge of Wellow Park to a road.

2.   Turn right onto the road and walk uphill. At the end of the woodland ignore the first bridleway to the right and continue to the second 200 metres further on.

3.   Turn right onto a track and walk across a field with a ditch on your right. The path leads into woodland and soon begins to follow the edge of the wood. Eventually the path bends to the right around a field corner.

4.   Go through a gate and turn left onto a track, which heads gently downhill and bends to the left. When the track bends to the right to Jordan Castle Farm continue ahead through a gate. The path leads to the A616.

5.   Turn right and follow the road through Wellow and back to the Dam.

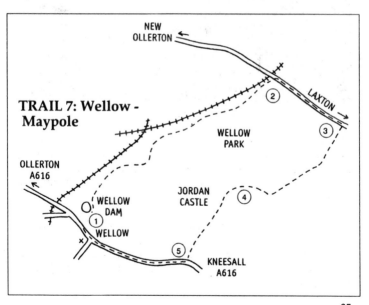

TRAIL 8: Kirton

Distance:	11.25 kilometres/7 miles
Start:	Whitewater Lane in between the A614 and Walesby on a corner close to a T-junction and a scout camp
Maps:	OS Sherwood Forest Explorer 28
	OS Pathfinder 763 (SK67/77) Clumber Park and East Markham
	OS Pathfinder 780 (SK66/76) Ollerton
Refreshments:	Public house in Kirton
Toilets:	None
Key features:	A section of the Robin Hood Way and Kirton

Kirton features two seventeenth century farmhouses and a church, which is mainly thirteenth century.

Walesby is home of the International Scout Camp.

This walk adds little to our knowledge of the history of the area, but it has been included because the countryside is very pleasant and on a clear day the views are extensive.

ROUTE INSTRUCTIONS

1. Turn left onto the road and head diagonally across a T-junction to a signpost. The wide track runs diagonally through Boughton Brake. Ignore all side turnings until you eventually reach a junction of tracks by some railings at the edge of the wood. Turn left onto the signposted public bridleway and walk with the edge of the wood on your left and fields on your right until you reach a lane.

2. Turn right and cross a railway. As the road bends sharply to the left a signpost points you in the same direction across several fields to a road. Cross the road and pass through a gate. Turn right and then left to follow the field edge. When you reach a gate on your right pass through the gate and head straight over the field to a gate at the other side. Turn left and in 75 metres pass through another gate and then immediately climb a stile on your right. Head over to a large farm gate. Keep to the field edge on your left after passing through this gate to a stile. Climb the stile and turn left to climb another stile in 10 metres. Follow a field edge with the hedge on your left to the A6075 at Kirton.

3.   Turn left on to the road, passing a museum. At the church the road bends sharply to the right. Take the side turn to the left and after 100 metres turn left over a stile at a signpost. Walk down to a gate and pick up a track in between a wire fence on each side. Follow this to a stile. Climb the stile and follow the field edge with the hedge on your right to another stile. Climb this stile and continue along the field edge. At the end of this field join a track hedged on both sides to a T-junction of roads.

4.   Turn left heading towards Walesby. At a stile by a signpost turn right virtually opposite Willoughby Sawmill. Walk along a field edge with a fence on the left to a stile. Climb the stile and keep ahead until you reach a footbridge over Bevercotes Beck. Turn left and follow the public bridleway across a green lane, where you join the Robin Hood Way, and continue to a road.

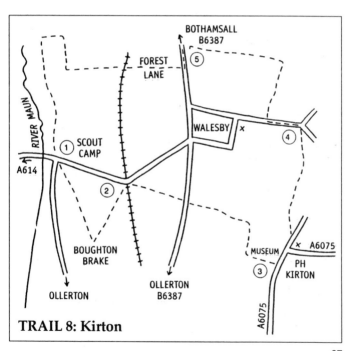

TRAIL 8: Kirton

5. Turn left to leave the Robin Hood Way and then right onto a public bridleway called Forest Lane. At the end of the lane continue in the same direction through a gate and on to a track. The track passes over a railway line and eventually turns sharp right. At a T-junction of tracks turn left to rejoin the Robin Hood Way and enter woodland. At a junction of tracks turn left. Initially the River Maun is 50 metres over to the right, but you move closer to it later on. After 10 metres cross a gravel track and then follow a clear path frequently marked with posts. *Along here lies Robin Hood's Cave in an outcrop of bunter sandstone, although there is little to see.* The path returns you to the road and your starting point.

Bess of Hardwick Country

TRAIL 9: Hardwick Hall

Distance:	10.5 kilometres/6.5 miles
Start:	Hardwick Country Park - Hardwick Ponds
Maps:	OS Pathfinder 779 (SK46/56) Mansfield (North) & part of Sherwood Forest
Refreshments:	None, unless visiting Hardwick Hall
Toilets:	Hardwick Ponds car park
Key features:	Hardwick Hall, The Old Hall, Ault Hucknall Church, the Rowthorne Trail, a section of the Teversal Trail and Hardwick Ponds

Bess of Hardwick - Elizabeth, Countess of Shrewsbury, better known by her nickname, Bess of Hardwick, was a formidable landowner and businesswoman who was born in 1527 and died at the age of 80 in 1608. She was the daughter of a Derbyshire squire who owned a small manor house in Hardwick. She married four times, each time to a husband more wealthy and influential than the last, and she outlived them all to become the richest and most powerful woman in England after Queen Elizabeth I.

In 1583 she bought the Hardwick property from her bankrupt brother. At this time Bess was married, although separated, from her fourth and last husband, the 6th Earl of Shrewsbury, who was head of one of the oldest and richest families in England and is often remembered for his guardianship of Mary Queen of Scots.

Hardwick Old Hall - Initially Bess pooled her resources into rebuilding the manor house as the present Hardwick Old Hall. However, the death of the Earl transformed her financial position and within a matter of weeks she commissioned the building of Hardwick Hall within yards of the Old Hall. Remains of the incomplete Old Hall still survive today in the hands of English Heritage.

Hardwick Hall - Bess moved into the largely completed new hall in

Hardwick Hall and The Old Hall from Hardwick Ponds

1597, which was almost certainly designed by Robert Smythson. Standing on top of a windblown scarp Hardwick Hall, "more glass than wall," is one of the finest and most complete examples of Elizabethan architecture with an emphasis on symmetry that history and chance have miraculously preserved. Its majestic qualities led to it being regarded by contemporaries as a masterpiece of innovative features and ingenious design. Undoubtedly it was built to reflect the wealth and status of Bess with six imposing towers and the huge initials ES crowning the roofline. Unusually for the time the building also contained a vast area of windows and glass. Glass was an expensive material of the day and to use it on such a scale was a display of extravagance.

Hardwick survives today with many of its original contents as listed in an inventory taken in 1601. It has a unique antiquarian atmosphere and has escaped modernisation, without being left neglected, in the hands of the Cavendish family (the current Dukes of Devonshire) until 1959, when it was accepted in lieu of Death Duties and handed over to the National Trust.

The Hardwick Inn - The inn is situated at the edge of the park on the banks of the River Doe. It was built by John Painter and as a reward for his long and loyal service to Bess he was allowed to live there rent free as its first landlord. His real name was John Ballechous, but as a painter by trade and due to the difficulties of spelling his name, he was known as John Painter in the estate records. John was responsible for much of the decoration at Hardwick and he also made important decisions about the construction.

Ault Hucknall Church - The tiny parish Church of St John the Baptist at Ault Hucknall is of Norman and Saxon origin and contains a monument to the first Countess of Devonshire designed by John Smythson. There is also a floor slab marking the burial place of the seventeenth century political philosopher Thomas Hobbes, who was tutor to the son of Sir William Cavendish at Chatsworth House.

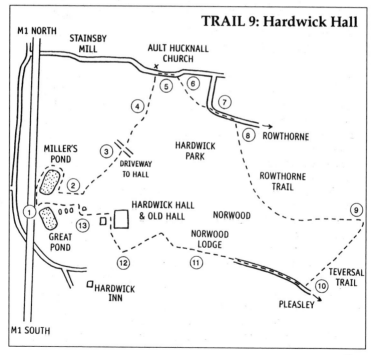

TRAIL 9: Hardwick Hall

ROUTE INSTRUCTIONS

1.	Start from the information point / toilet block and take the path to the left around Miller Pond. Follow the path around the pond and shortly after passing through a second kissing gate turn left at a crossroad of paths.

2.	When you see a gate and kissing gate in front of you, look to the left for another kissing gate and go through it. Follow the gentle uphill path to another kissing gate in the top left-hand corner of the field.

3.	Go through this gate and cross over the road and continue ahead between trees. For the first 100 metres a path cannot be seen on the ground, but if you keep roughly half way between the road on the right and the fence on the left a small marker post comes into view. A path then becomes visible and as you continue to climb it begins to swing to the left to a kissing gate in front of a cottage.

4.	Follow the well-surfaced track to a lane. Ault Hucknall church can be seen on the lane.

5.	Turn right onto the lane and after 200 metres turn right through a gate.

6.	Take the right-hand fork across a field to a stile. Climb the stile and cross a second field to another stile. After crossing the stile turn right onto a lane.

7.	Ignore the right fork, which leads to Hardwick Hall and follow the road round to the left, signposted Rowthorne, for several hundred metres.

8.	Turn right into the Rowthorne Trail car park and after 50 metres take the track to the left signposted "The Trail". Follow the trail across a number of stiles for 2 kilometres until you reach a lane.

9.	At the lane take the right fork and climb a stile immediately in front of you. Turn right and follow a section of the Teversal Trail to a lane.

10.	Turn right onto the lane and follow it towards a sprinkling of houses on the right. *It is here that the gamekeeper Oliver Mellors lived in D.H. Lawrence's* Lady Chatterley's Lover. Pass the Norwood Lodge. After the last house the lane becomes a rough track. Follow it to a gate and turn right over a stile.

11.   The path passes through Lady Spencer's Wood to a stile. Cross the stile and follow the path ahead across a field to a kissing gate and onto a driveway of the Hardwick Estate.

12.   Turn right and walk uphill crossing a cattlegrid and soon reaching the Old Hall on the left and Hardwick Hall on the right. Almost opposite the entrance to Hardwick Hall a downhill path can be seen 50 metres to the left. Follow the path through a kissing gate and continue downhill to another kissing gate in the fence on your right just after the first Row Pond.

13.   Follow the path between the first and second Row Pond and turn left to follow the edge of the pond. (Ignore the clearer track ahead.) Follow the edge of another pond and then continue to the Great Pond. Go through a kissing gate and cross a footbridge before arriving back at the car park. *Before leaving the Great Pond turn around for a magnificent view of both the Old Hall and Hardwick Hall.*

Pilgrim Father Country

TRAIL 10: Babworth Church

Distance:	14.5 kilometres/9 miles
Start:	Churchgate long stay car park in Retford town centre - next to the bridge on the A620 over the River Idle
Maps:	OS Pathfinder 745 (SK68/78) East Retford (North) & Blyth
	OS Pathfinder 763 (SK67/77) Clumber Park & East Markham
Refreshments:	Public houses and cafes in Retford
Toilets:	Retford, but none along the route
Key features:	A section of the Cuckoo Way and Babworth church

Retford - To the west of the River Idle lies the oldest part of Retford, which clusters around the ancient St Michael's Church. Over to the east of the river a twelfth century charter created a market town. This market town rose to its heyday of prosperity when the Great North Road, the modern day A1, was built in 1776 originally through the centre of Retford. This was quickly followed by the completion of the Chesterfield Canal in 1777, which also runs through the town. The building of a railway in 1849 then created further impact. Retford has many charming buildings, including a Victorian town hall surrounded by stately Georgian houses.

The Pilgrim Fathers - It is strange to think that the origins of some of the early settlers in the United States of America can be traced back to sleepy rural North Nottinghamshire. However, the villages around Retford are where many of The Pilgrim Fathers had their roots.

When the son of Mary Queen of Scots, James VI of Scotland, became James I of England in the early sixteenth century many English Protestants were persecuted for their Puritan beliefs and their refusal to conform to the king's rules on religion. One group of religious dissenters, the Separatists, who later became known as the Pilgrims, decided to emigrate so that they could hopefully live and

44

worship in peace. In 1620 approximately one hundred Pilgrims and their families set sail from Plymouth on a cargo ship called *The Mayflower*. They planned a journey to the New World and embarked upon a treacherous and stormy voyage across the Atlantic Ocean, which cost many of them their lives. The survivors eventually landed in New England and formed the colony of Massachusetts.

Babworth - The 700-year-old Babworth church, which stands close to the parklands of the eighteenth century Babworth Hall, has strong connections with The Pilgrim Fathers. It was here that the dissenting sermons of Richard Clifton provided the inspiration and laid the foundation of the Pilgrim movement.

Scrooby was the home of the leader of the Pilgrims, William Brewster.

Austerfield is the birthplace of William Bradford. William later became a Governor of Plymouth, New England.

ROUTE INSTRUCTIONS

1. In the far corner of the long stay car park is a blue sign for the Market Place. This sign takes you out of the car park under an archway. At the road cross over and turn right across a bridge spanning the River Idle. At the end of the bridge turn left onto a riverside path through parkland with the river on your left. Turn left over the first bridge and then right to walk with the river on your right. At the next bridge turn right to walk over the bridge. On meeting the Chesterfield Canal climb down some steps onto the canal towpath and continue ahead.

2. This delightful stretch of the canal passes under bridges 55, 54B and 54A. Bridge 54 is Ladybridge under Sutton Lane. Continue along the towpath passing the various Forest locks and finally Forest Lock House. *These locks were once known as the Sherwood Forest Locks as they were just inside the boundary of the original forest.* From Forest Lock House to bridge 53 under the Old London Road the towpath is surfaced. *Up until a few hundred years ago this road carried the Great North Road until it was diverted through Retford town centre.*

3. Leave the canal at bridge 52. Turn left onto Green Mile Lane, which is a green lane planted with an avenue of trees on both sides. Cross over the A620 and continue ahead. After passing the second

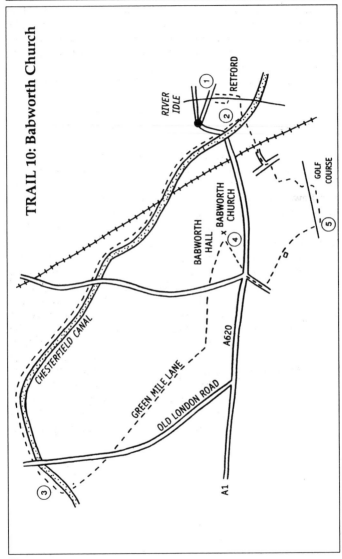

TRAIL 10: Babworth Church

plantation of trees on your left there is a public footpath sign to the left for Babworth church. At the end of the plantation climb a stile in front of you. Walk across the middle of a small field to another stile. Climb this and head across a field keeping to the left of a small circle of trees to another stile. Cross over Sutton Lane and follow the signpost across the middle of another field to a stile. The path now brings you to Babworth church. *Along the way the remains of Babworth Hall can be seen on the left. John Simpson transformed this thirteenth century property in the eighteenth century and Humphrey Repton landscaped the grounds.*

4.   Turn right onto a surfaced lane by the gateway to Haygarth House. This lane leads to the junction of the A620 and B6420. Cross over and walk up the right-hand side of the B6420 for 150 metres. At a bridleway sign on your left follow the winding surfaced lane to Great Morton Farm. Continue past the farm on what is now a rough track. After passing under a railway bridge turn immediately left to walk with the railway on your left.

5.   This track leads onto a golf course. Continue in the same direction with care up the left-hand edge of the golf course to a footbridge over the railway. After crossing the footbridge you are faced with a selection of paths. Take the second path on your right through the trees. At a lane cross over and walk along the perimeter of a sports field. At the corner turn right along another edge of the field which leads to Ordsall Road. Turn left and in 50 metres turn right onto Ordsall Park Road. At a T-junction head over the large railway footbridge in front of you. Keep ahead along Pelham Lane, which leads to the bridge where you joined the Chesterfield Canal. Cross the bridge and retrace your steps to the bridge where you left the River Idle. Turn left and follow the riverside path on this side back to a supermarket car park. Walk through the car park and retrace your steps back to the Church Gate car park.

Bolsover Castle

TRAIL 11: Bolsover Castle -
Duke of Newcastle, 1st Creation

Distance:	11.25 kilometres/7 miles
Start:	Castle Street car park in Bolsover, almost opposite the entrance to the castle
Maps:	OS Pathfinder 779 (SK46/56) Mansfield (North) & part of Sherwood Forest
Refreshments:	Public house in Bolsover, Scarcliffe, Upper Langwith and Palterton
Toilets:	None unless visiting Bolsover Castle
Key features:	Bolsover Castle and a section of the Creswell Archaeological Way

The present **Bolsover Castle** stands dramatically at the top of a hill dominating the landscape for miles around. However, despite its commanding position, it is very much a castle in name only. The remains are those of an early seventeenth century mansion, built on the site of a twelfth century castle, in which all three generations of the Smythson architectural family probably had a hand. Within the grounds you will find the 'Little Castle', which is a richly decorated family suite within a self-contained 'keep', a now roofless terrace range and an indoor riding school.

The mood of the castle has been encapsulated by many. In his masque *Loves Welcome To Bolsover*, written for the visit of Charles I, Ben Johnson reminds us: "This is not a warlike place, much of its imagery is intellectual, sensual and designed to evoke the virtues of romantic love".

The manor of Bolsover was given by William The Conqueror to William Peverel I. The Peverel family's other castle at Castleton was very similar. By the end of the fourteenth century the castle had fallen out of use, although it remained in Royal hands until 1553 when it was granted to Sir George Talbot, the 6th Earl of Shrewsbury and the fourth husband of Bess of Hardwick. Charles Cavendish, a

Vicar Pond (Trail 5)
Hardwick Hall (Trail 9)

son of Bess by an earlier marriage, leased the Bolsover estate from the 7th Earl of Shrewsbury. Charles employed Robert Smythson to transform Bolsover, although both died before work had progressed very far.

In 1617 the heir to Bolsover was the son of Charles, William Cavendish. William was a well-known Royalist, a skilled horseman and an authority on equitation. He later became the 1st Duke of Newcastle of the 1st Creation and was known as the Horsemanship Duke.

William, with the help of John Smythson, then continued where his father had left off. Effectively two houses were built, one a dream romantic folly with lavish interior decoration and the other a terrace range with grand staterooms for entertaining and accommodating important guests. William, who also resided at Welbeck, where he had built one of the earliest riding schools, then also built another riding school at Bolsover, probably with the assistance of Huntingdon Smythson.

After the civil war the Duke was forced into exile. In Antwerp he established another riding school and published the famous *Nouvelle Methode de Dresser les Chevaux* in 1658. He returned after the restoration and died in 1676.

By the 1740s Welbeck had become very much the principal residence of the heirs and the castle was now unlived in. From 1755 to 1945 the castle was in the hands of the Portland family, who transferred it to the nation. The castle is now looked after by English Heritage.

ROUTE INSTRUCTIONS

1.   Turn left out of the car park exit onto High Street. Pass the Blue Bell Inn on your right and the church on your left. Turn right onto Langwith Road and after 400 metres turn right at a crossroads onto Mansfield Road.

2.   Just after the West View Hotel turn left at a public footpath sign and walk diagonally across the sports field to the far right-hand corner. Here a clear path takes you across two fields. As you enter the third field keep to the left side of the mound and continue straight ahead until you reach a track. On reaching the track look immediately over to the right for a path across a small field to a stile.

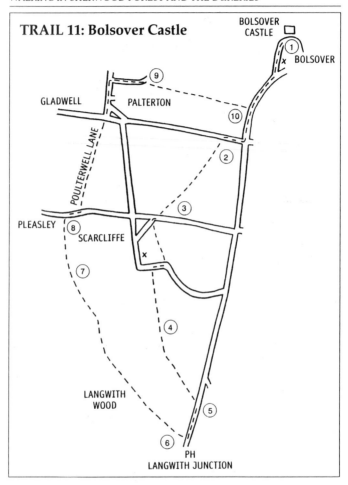

TRAIL 11: Bolsover Castle

BOLSOVER CASTLE

(1)

BOLSOVER

(9)

GLADWELL   PALTERTON

(10)

POULTERWELL LANE

(2)

(3)

PLEASLEY   (8)

SCARCLIFFE

(7)

(4)

LANGWITH WOOD

(5)

(6)

PH

LANGWITH JUNCTION

Climb the stile and continue across the next field to a road.

3.   Cross over the road and after a few metres turn left over a stile into a field. Turn right and in the field corner turn left to walk in the same direction, crossing several stiles, to join a lane on a corner. Turn right and just after a bus stop on your left and before Rock

House turn left onto a track.

4.   When the track ends, follow the field edge, keeping the hedge on your left-hand side, to a stile. Cross the stile and continue downhill to another stile in the fence by a road.

5.   Turn right and follow the road towards Upper Langwith. On reaching the brow of a hill, and as The Devonshire Arms comes into view, double back to the right at a signpost onto a path, which is part of the Creswell Archaeological Way.

6.   The path runs alongside a plantation before entering Langwith Wood. At the far end of the wood you reach a junction of tracks. Turn left and after 150 metres turn right just in front of some trees onto another track and leave the Creswell Archaeological Way.

7.   The track takes you into the edge of Roseland Wood. Shortly after entering the wood take the left-hand fork and continue to a stile. Climb the stile and walk along the edge of a field with the hedge on your right to a road.

8.   Turn right onto the road and after 100 metres turn left onto a green lane called Poulterwell Lane. Follow this track to a road. Cross the road and continue ahead into Palterton on Main Street. Main Street turns sharply to the right and is signposted Sutton Scarsdale.

9.   After 200 metres take the second of two right turns and continue ahead on a lane. The lane soon ends and you pass through a kissing gate onto a grassy track. Continue to a stile, passing farm buildings on your right. Climb the stile and follow the clearly defined track into a housing area. Continue in the same direction until you rejoin Langwith Road.

10.   Here turn left and retrace your steps, taking the left turn back onto High Street.

TRAIL 12: Scarcliffe

Distance:	8 kilometres/5 miles
Start:	A layby on Rotherham Road in between Scarcliffe and Stony Houghton close to Birch Hill Plantation
Maps:	OS Pathfinder 779 (SK46/56) Mansfield (North) & part of Sherwood Forest

Refreshments:	Public houses in Scarcliffe
Toilets:	None
Key features:	Scarcliffe church and a section of the Creswell Archaeological Way

ROUTE INSTRUCTIONS

1.   From the layby and facing the road turn right. After 100 metres, opposite a green lane called Poulterwell Lane, take the second right onto a public footpath into Birch Hill Plantation. Near the edge of the woodland watch out carefully for a fork off to the left leading to a stile in a wall 10 metres away. Climb the stile and diagonally cross a field to another stile. Cross the stile and turn left onto Gang Lane, which is hedged on both sides.

2.   On reaching a lane turn right and walk through Scarcliffe village passing St Leonard's Church on your left. *This late twelfth/*

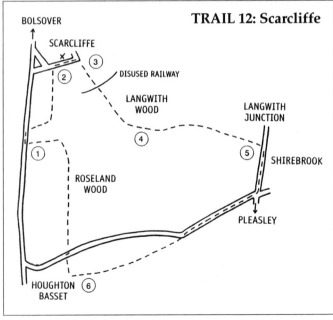

early thirteenth century listed building houses the tomb of Constantina Frechville, who died around 1200. The tomb shows Constantina holding a baby. According to legend she lost her way in Scarcliffe Wood and used the ringing church bells to help her find her way back out again. She left five acres of land when she died and the rent from this paid for the curfew bell to be rung three weeks before Christmas and three weeks after. This tradition is still carried out today. Just before reaching a public house and Station Road on a sharp left-hand bend, turn right onto a public footpath.

3.   Pass a house called The Birches on your left and reach a stile in front of you. Climb the stile and follow a field edge with the hedge on your right. The path bends to the right over a disused railway line and follows a field edge to a footbridge. Cross the footbridge and enter Langwith Wood. On reaching a T-junction with a track turn right.

4.   At a triangular junction turn right and then left at a T-junction after several metres. This wide track follows the edge of the wood with the trees on your left. Shortly after passing the end of the woodland you are faced with a choice of three paths. Take the middle path, which diagonally crosses the middle of several fields before reaching a road on the outskirts of Shirebrook.

5.   Cross over the road to the pavement on the opposite side and turn right. At a crossroads by Harrisons Nursery turn right. The road heads uphill with a cemetery on the left. At the end of the buildings for Stony Houghton Reservoir Booster Station on your right there is a series of green lanes on the left by an electrical substation. Take the track hedged on both sides called Balkham Lane to the right of the substation and join the Creswell Archaeological Way. This lane later becomes Water Lane and it can become quite muddy at certain times of the year.

6.   On reaching farm buildings on your right climb a stile in the wall in between the buildings. Head uphill to a stile. Climb the stile and turn right onto a lane for a few metres. Turn left onto a wide track and keep straight ahead at a fork heading for the corner of Roseland Wood. Follow the edge of the wood and keep straight ahead at a T-junction to leave the Creswell Archaeological Way. On reaching a hedge with a stile over to the right turn left to follow a field edge back to the layby.

The Dukeries

THORESBY HALL

The acquisition of Thoresby by the 3rd Earl of Kingston made it the principal seat of the Pierreponts. The 5th Earl, whose mother was a daughter of Bess of Hardwick, was elevated to the 1st Duke of Kingston upon Hull in the early seventeenth century, although the dukedom became extinct in 1773 when the 2nd Duke died. His heir was his nephew Charles Meadows, who adopted the name and arms of the Pierreponts. In 1807 he was created 1st Earl of Manvers.

The present Victorian mansion, the third house to be built, was one of the last great houses to be built in England by the 3rd Earl of Manvers and the fashionable architect Anthony Salvin. It was a showpiece of Victorian concepts with two estate villages nearby. To the west lie the Gothic houses of Budby. Perlethorpe stands to the east with its charming little church.

The title of the Earl of Manvers became extinct upon the death of the 6th Earl in 1958. The house is not open to the public and remains a private property.

A statue in the grounds of Rufford

TRAIL 13: Rufford Abbey - The Savi

Distance:	8 kilometres/5 miles
Start:	Rufford Abbey Country Park
Maps:	OS Sherwood Forest Explorer 28
	OS Pathfinder 780 (SK66/76) Ollerton
Refreshments:	Country park and public houses in Edwinstowe
Toilets:	Country park
Key features:	Rufford Abbey, Rufford Mill and a section of the Robin Hood Way

Rufford Abbey is usually geographically included as part of the Dukeries, although no owner ever achieved a dukedom. Standing at the entrance gates looking down lime avenue you could be forgiven for thinking that this once great house, said to be one of the most haunted houses in England, was still standing. In reality all that remains is a shell providing an ornamental feature to what is now a country park.

In the twelfth century wealthy families often gave generously to religious orders. Gilbert De Gant, the Earl of Lincoln, founded a Cistercian Abbey, as a 'daughter' house to Rievaulx Abbey in Yorkshire, at Rufford.

After the dissolution in 1536 the estate was granted in 1537 to George Talbot the 4th Earl of Shrewsbury. It was the 6th Earl and fourth husband of Bess of Hardwick who was to transform the abbey into a large country house. Despite the fact that Rufford was one of the Shrewsbury estates that Bess did not acquire, she still managed to leave her mark on its history.

Bess was well known for ambitious schemes for her children and so she arranged the secret marriage of her daughter Elizabeth to the Earl of Lennox, the brother-in-law of Mary Queen of Scots and fifth in line to the throne, at Rufford. This act caused the break-up of her marriage to the 6th Earl of Shrewsbury, who was a deeply patriotic man. The young married couple both died shortly afterwards, leaving an only child, Lady Arabella Stuart. Lady Arabella was to lead a tragic life, as her royal blood in the power game of politics and the monarchy led to her imprisonment and death in the Tower of London.

The 7th Earl, Gilbert, married Bess's daughter Mary Cavendish. Gilbert often entertained the Protestant King James I, who liked hunting in Sherwood Forest. However, Gilbert had an uneasy relationship with the King as Mary became a Roman Catholic and the King's soldiers often searched Rufford.

In 1626 the house passed from the Shrewburys to the Savilles, who were wealthy Yorkshire landowners. The 3rd baronet, Sir William Saville, unstintingly pledged his support to Charles I when the Civil War broke out in 1642 and in recognition of his skills as a military commander he was made Governor of York and then Sheffield. He even ordered his principal home at Thornhill to be burned down so that the Parliamentary forces could not capture it. When he died, his widow, the day before she gave birth, personally directed the siege of Sheffield Castle against the Roundheads, although she was eventually forced to surrender.

The heir to Sir William the Cavalier was Sir George and he is probably the most famous of the Savilles and arguably deserved a dukedom. As a loyal Royalist he almost certainly played a leading part in a failed plot to put Charles II back on the throne and to overthrow Cromwell. In recognition of his loyalty, Sir George became 1st Marquess of Halifax in 1685. As an unbiased and patriotic statesman he became known as 'The Trimmer'. He also made great improvements to the mansion at Rufford. When the 2nd Marquess died the peerage became extinct.

The 8th baronet was another distinguished politician. If his advice had been taken over the American colonies, it is possible the War of Independence could have been avoided. With no heirs the baronet's inheritance passed on instruction in his will to the second son of his sister on the basis that he took the name of Saville. Richard Lumley Saville eventually became the 6th Earl of Scarborough.

It was the 8th Earl of Scarborough who used the services of Anthony Salvin, who designed Thorseby Hall, to extend Rufford in the 1830s. The 8th Earl also created the lime tree drive and wrought iron gates at the entrance. He rescued a French girl from drowning in London's Serpentine and although they never married she lived at Rufford and produced five sons and one daughter.

The 8th Earl's inheritance passed to his second son, Captain Henry Saville Lumley. He was a keen racehorse owner and his horse Cremorne, which won the Derby in 1872 and the Ascot Gold in 1873, is buried on the Rufford Estate.

John Saville Lumley, in recognition of a long and distinguished diplomatic career, was created 1st Baron Saville. When the 2nd Baron Saville died in 1931, the 3rd Baron was still only a minor and by 1938 rising taxes and expenses forced his trustees to sell the Rufford Estate.

After several owners the army took over the estate during World War II and then the Civil Defence until the early 1950s when the estate passed into the hands of Nottinghamshire Council. In 1969 Rufford became a designated country park and the remaining buildings are in the hands of English Heritage.

ROUTE INSTRUCTIONS

1.   From the car park follow the path signposted to the Abbey. Turn left in front of the stable block and walk past the Abbey's remains on your right. Continue ahead along a wide path lined with trees. This path turns at a right angle. At a T-junction turn left and

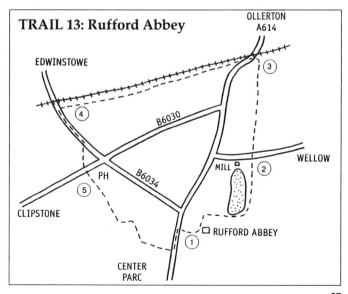

TRAIL 13: Rufford Abbey

Rufford lake

then right at a crossroad of tracks. This clear path takes you across several bridges and then up the right-hand side of the lake. The old mill complex can be seen at the far end of the lake.

2.   After passing the lake you reach a stile. Climb it and cross the road. A path opposite takes you along a field edge. Initially the hedge is on your left, although as you continue in the same direction the hedge will be on your right.

3.   You emerge onto the A614 by a railway bridge. Cross over the road and climb a stile. This path leads to a footbridge, which spans Rainworth Water, and shortly after the bridge there is a stile on your left. Climb the stile and turn right. Continue in the same direction along the edge of fields, with a fence and a railway line on your right, into Edwinstowe.

4.   On reaching the B6034 turn left. Ten metres after passing Sandy Lane on your right, a signpost marks a path off to your right in between a fence and a hedge. Cross a road and pass the South Forest leisure centre on your left.

5.   Cross over the B6030 and take the path opposite, to join the Robin Hood Way, along a field edge with the hedge on your left. The

path leads into woodland for 50 metres. At the end of the trees turn left and follow a field edge. This path bends to the right and leads to a T-junction. Turn left onto the wide track. When you meet a surfaced lane continue in the same direction along another track for 100 metres to the A624. Turn left and then right back into the car park.

TRAIL 14: Worksop Manor - The Dukes of Norfolk

Distance:	13 kilometres/8 miles
Start:	Hannah Park car park opposite the Lion Gate built as an entrance to the Welbeck Estate
Maps:	OS Sherwood Forest Explorer 28
	OS Pathfinder 762 (SK47/57) Staveley & Worksop (South)
	OS Pathfinder 762 (SK67/77) Clumber Park & East Markham
Refreshments:	None
Toilets:	None
Key features:	Worksop Manor, a section of the Robin Hood Way, the edges of Clumber Park and the Welbeck Estate

There was a time when **Worksop Manor** was one of the largest and grandest mansions in the north of England, although now all that remains of the 500 room building is a relatively small private house owned by the Farr family.

Following the Norman Conquest, the Manor of Worksop passed through Roger de Busli, the de Lovetots and the Furnival family. Maud Baroness Furnival married Sir John Talbot, who became 1st Earl of Shrewsbury.

The property remained in the hands of the Earls of Shrewsbury for quite some time. The 6th Earl and fourth husband of Bess of Hardwick imprisoned Mary Queen of Scots in Worksop Manor twice in 1570 whilst she was in his guardianship. Following the marriage of the 7th Earl's daughter the mansion passed to the Howards.

In 1761 the house was burned to the ground. The owner at that time was the 7th Duke of Norfolk who started to rebuild Worksop Manor in the Palladian style. The subsequent Dukes of Norfolk neglected the property and it was eventually sold to the 4th Duke of Newcastle. However, as he did not need another large house near to Clumber he pulled much of it down.

In 1890 the estate was sold to Sir Thomas Robinson and was inherited by his great nephew, Captain John Farr, whose family are the present owners.

ROUTE INSTRUCTIONS

1. Leave the car park on a path between a gap in the fence into the woodland and keep following the right-hand edge of the wood until you emerge onto the B6034 just above the far end of the wood.

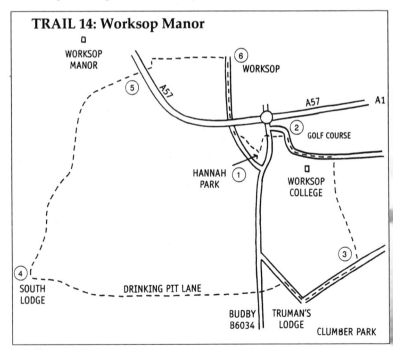

Cross the road and head through a gap in the hedge into woodland and continue in the same direction until you reach the Old Coach Road.

2. Turn right, passing Worksop Golf Club on your left and Worksop College on your right. Turn right onto a public bridleway signposted for Hardwick village. Continue ahead at a crossroads and then ahead again at the next crossroads, which takes you diagonally across the golf course. The path then takes you into woodland and to a cottage. Turn right at a T-junction and keep right at the fork in front of you, following a clear wide track to a road.

3. Turn right onto the Robin Hood Way and at a T-junction with Truman's Lodge on your left turn right. Look out for a public bridleway signpost on your left. Follow the track to the B6034. Cross the road and continue ahead on Drinking Pit Lane. Pass two old lodges on your left and eventually head down a gorge to South Lodge where you leave the Robin Hood Way.

4. Turn right at a sign for "Worksop 2 miles". *Before turning right look to your left to see the blocked up entrance to one of the Duke of Portland's tunnels.* In 50 metres at a T-junction turn left and follow a track, at first through woodland and then into open country. As you reach the open, Worksop Manor can be seen ahead. Continue along the clear track keeping ahead at a crossroad of tracks. A hundred metres later turn right over a stile. Follow the field edge with the hedge on your right to the A57.

5. Carefully cross over the road and down some steps. Turn left and follow the path as it turns to the right. Turn left at a T-junction and soon you reach a road. Turn left and then take the first right onto Robinson Drive.

6. Turn right at a T-junction onto Sparken Hill. This road crosses back over the A57. When the houses end on your left turn left into Hannah Park. Go through a gap in a fence and head uphill heading in the same direction back to the car park.

TRAIL 15: Worksop Manor Lodge and Shireoaks Hall

Distance:	12 kilometres/7.5 miles
Start:	Roadside parking, next to the old colliery terraced houses, on Shireoaks Row in the village of Shireoaks, between the railway line and the church
Maps:	OS Pathfinder 762 (SK47/57) Staveley & Worksop (South)
	OS Pathfinder 744 (SK48/58) Aughton & Carlton in Lindrick
Refreshments:	The Hewitt Arms in Shireoaks
Toilets:	None
Key features:	Worksop Manor Lodge, Shireoaks Hall and the village of Shireoaks

Shireoaks is mentioned as a Domesday village. The Dukes of Newcastle, from the Clumber Estate, built both the church and the colliery housing. Indeed, it was the Duke of Newcastle who sank the first deep pit colliery in Nottinghamshire at Shireoaks in 1845.

ROUTE INSTRUCTIONS

1.   Walk to the Church of St Luke the Evangelist on your left-hand side. At the T-junction turn right soon, crossing the River Ryton. Turn left onto the driveway for The Hewitt Arms. *This public house is a converted early eighteenth century coach house in the grounds of Shireoaks Hall.* Walk in front of The Hewitt Arms and at the end of the lake on your left turn right at a fork. This path bends to the left and passes in between the remains of Shireoaks Hall on your left and a manmade ornamental stretch of water on your right. *Although no documentary evidence survives to indicate when the hall was built, its design, which is closely related to that of Bolsover's Little Castle, suggests that it can be reasonably ascribed to John Smythson in the early seventeenth century.*

2.   At a junction by a gate turn right onto a track to walk with a fence and later a hedge on your left. Pass through a gate and turn right to head across the middle of a field to another gate. The track

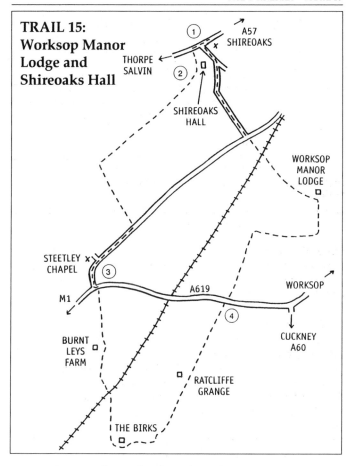

**TRAIL 15:
Worksop Manor
Lodge and
Shireoaks Hall**

① A57 SHIREOAKS

THORPE SALVIN ←
② SHIREOAKS HALL

WORKSOP MANOR LODGE

STEETLEY ✗ CHAPEL
③
M1
A619
④
WORKSOP
CUCKNEY A60

BURNT LEYS FARM
RATCLIFFE GRANGE
THE BIRKS

now continues with woodland on your right and then back out into open country. At a crossroad of tracks turn left over a stile. Walk across the middle of a field and then keep in the same direction along the edge of the next field. Turn right onto a lane and follow this to the A619. *Before reaching the main road at a T-junction by Steetley Farm, the small secluded Norman architectural gem of Steetley chapel can*

A pond next to the Hewitt Arms

be seen over to your right. Built in 1120 the chapel is regarded as having a high architectural value, in particular for its doorway. Prior to its restoration in 1880 by J. Pearson it had become derelict and was used for cockfighting and as a sheepfold.

3.   On reaching the A619 cross over and continue ahead up the driveway to Burnt Leys Farm. The track heads past the farm and becomes a rough track close to some large gates. After 150 metres the track bends to the right, but your route bears to the left across the middle of a field and under a railway bridge. The trail then heads over a number of fields from stile to stile. When you reach a field with The Birks Farmhouse on your left pass over another stile out of that field and then head diagonally across the next field to a stile in the far left-hand corner of the field. Cross the stile and join a track. In 20 metres turn left at a T-junction and walk towards the farmhouse. Look out for a stile on your right. Cross this stile and then another shortly afterwards to join a track. A hundred metres further on you climb a stile and walk in between The Birks Cottages. The bridleway then bends to the left with distant glimpses of Worksop Manor over to your right. Pass Ratcliffe cottages and Ratcliffe Grange on your left, before you eventually emerge back onto the A619.

4.   Cross over and join a track on the opposite side of the road. As the track bends to the left by a white house, turn right over a stile. Just before a stile, turn right over a footbridge and follow a path

across the middle of three fields to a lane. Turn left onto the lane and walk in between a farm and Worksop Manor Lodge. *The lodge is now a public house. This tall building has many features which suggest it was designed by Robert Smythson for the Shrewsburys, after the completion of the nearby Worksop Manor.* Turn left at a T-junction opposite the side of the lodge. Pass under a railway bridge and emerge onto Steetley Lane at a T-junction. Continue ahead along the lane noting the interesting cottages and the old mill as you enter Shireoaks village. Turn left at the T-junction and return to the church.

TRAIL 16: The Welbeck Estate - The Dukes of Portland

Distance:	11.25 kilometres/7 miles
Start:	Creswell visitor centre car park
Maps:	OS Sherwood Forest Explorer 28
	OS Pathfinder 772 (SK47/57) Staveley & Worksop (South)
Refreshments:	Limited selection at visitor centre
Toilets:	Visitor centre
Key features:	Welbeck Estate, Worksop Manor and a section of the Robin Hood Way

Welbeck Abbey is now a military college and the estate is private property, with access strictly limited to the public footpath running through it. In its time it was a magnificent house with everything on a grand scale.

The Abbey was founded as a Premonstratensian house in 1153. However, after the dissolution the estate came into the possession of Gilbert Talbot, son of the 6th Earl of Shrewsbury and fourth husband of Bess of Hardwick, who was to become the 7th Earl. Later, Welbeck passed into the hands of a son of Bess of Hardwick by an earlier marriage, called Charles Cavendish. His son, William Cavendish, who was to become the 1st Duke of Newcastle of the 1st Creation, then inherited Welbeck. It was William who built the first riding school at Welbeck. Both Charles and William also have strong links with Bolsover Castle.

After several further changes in ownership the estate came into the hands of the Bentinck family in 1741 and it is still in their occupation. The Bentincks were titled the **Dukes of Portland** and are a well-known historical family. The 3rd Duke was the Prime Minister twice in George III's reign. However, it is the 5th Duke who is probably the most famous. He was an eccentric recluse and had miles of underground passages built around Welbeck, including an underground ballroom, which is the largest room in Europe without supporting pillars. He also built a replacement riding school at Welbeck and at that time, in terms of size, this was second only to the Spanish Riding School in Vienna.

The contrast with the 6th Duke was enormous, as suddenly the house became one of the great social centres of England. Following the death of the 7th Duke in 1977 the estate passed to his daughter Lady Anne Bentinck, who still lives on the estate.

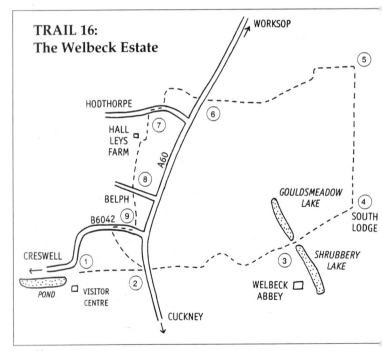

TRAIL 16:
The Welbeck Estate

ROUTE INSTRUCTIONS

1.   From the car park take the track, which is part of the Robin Hood Way, walking away from the visitor centre. Pass through a kissing gate and continue to the A60.

2.   Cross the road and follow the tarmac tree-lined lane ahead. At Oaksetts Lodge, which is on your right, continue ahead at a crossroad of tracks. The track bends to the left and then to the right. After a further 100 metres, at a signpost, turn off the tarmac track onto a path. On your right-hand side you pass trees, a sports field and then more trees until you reach a tarmac track. Turn right and look out for Gouldsmeadow Lake on your left. Shortly afterwards you come to a T-junction.

3.   Turn left and walk in between two lakes. A clear path continues ahead, which runs alongside a tunnel built by the eccentric 5th Duke of Portland. *Take care not to wander from the path, as the tunnel is still ventilated and not all the skylights are capped.*

4.   On reaching the South Lodge pass through a gate. Turn right and after 50 metres pass through another gate. Turn left and go through a metal gate and in another 50 metres, at a T-junction of tracks, turn left to leave the Robin Hood Way. After 20 metres turn right through a gate at a public footpath sign to Worksop. *Before turning right, look to your left to see the blocked up entrance to the tunnel.* In 50 metres, at a T-junction, turn left and follow a track at first through woodland and then into open country. As you reach the open, Worksop Manor can be seen ahead. Continue along the clear track until you reach a crossroad of tracks.

5.   Turn left onto a track hedged on both sides. At the end of the track turn left over a stile and follow the edge of a field. After 50 metres watch out carefully for a yellow waymarker indicating a path off to the right, which crosses a stream. Keeping the fields on your left follow the edge of two fields and then look out for a signpost off to the right. Cross a stile and continue along a field edge to a signpost in the middle of the field. Here turn left and walk across the middle of the field. At the end of the field continue ahead and cross a dried up stream and walk across the middle of another field to the A60.

6.   Cross the road and climb a stile. Walk across the middle of yet

another field to a stile. Cross the stile and continue ahead. After 100 metres the track bends to the left and leads down to a lane. Turn right onto the lane and after 100 metres turn left.

7.   Walk up towards Hall Leys Farm. The track bends to the right towards the farmhouse. Here at a signpost turn left to leave the lane and head across a field. Cross three fields in total before reaching a lane at Belph.

8.   Cross the lane and walk up the No Through Road. At a T-junction of tracks turn left and pass Lilac Cottage on your left. At a public footpath sign the track bends to the right and continues to a road.

9.   Turn right onto the B6042 and after 250 metres, as you reach the disused tip on your right, turn left onto a green lane, which is hedged on both sides. This lane leads to the A60. Turn right, and in 50 metres turn right again to retrace your steps to the car park.

TRAIL 17: The Welbeck Estate - The Dukes of Portland

Distance:	8 kilometres/5 miles
Start:	Cuckney church/village hall car park, Norton Lane
Maps:	OS Sherwood Forest Explorer 28
	OS Pathfinder 762 (SK47/57) Staveley & Worksop (South)
Refreshments:	The Greendale Oak at Cuckney
Toilets:	None
Key features:	The Welbeck Estate, Cuckney village and a section of the Robin Hood Way

ROUTE INSTRUCTIONS

1.   Turn left out of the car park and walk along the lane passing St Mary's Church on your left. Follow the lane around a sharp left-hand bend and into Norton, *winner of a number of Best Kept Village awards.*

2.   Turn left onto Infield Lane at a signpost for Holbeck and Worksop to join the Robin Hood Way. After 200 metres turn right

at a signpost. Climb the stile and follow a field edge with the hedge on the left. At the end of the field pass through a kissing gate.

3.   Turn left onto a surfaced track lined with trees on both sides. *Bunker's Hill Lodge, with its large wrought iron gates, can be seen at the entrance to the Welbeck Estate.* Pass Park Lodge on your right and enter Kiln Wood. At a T-junction of tracks turn right. At the next junction turn left to walk towards the A60.

4.   Cross the A60 and continue ahead on the lane into Holbeck Woodhouse. Just before you reach the houses, the Robin Hood Way turns to the right, but the trail keeps straight ahead. In Holbeck Woodhouse the lane bends sharply to the left at Garden Cottage. At a T-junction turn left and then immediately take the left fork in front

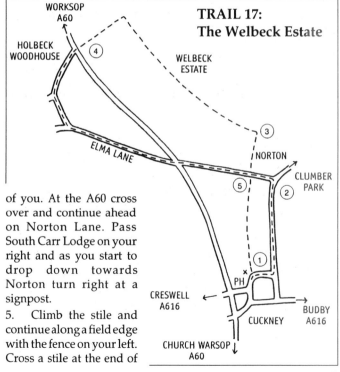

TRAIL 17:
The Welbeck Estate

of you. At the A60 cross over and continue ahead on Norton Lane. Pass South Carr Lodge on your right and as you start to drop down towards Norton turn right at a signpost.

5.   Climb the stile and continue along a field edge with the fence on your left. Cross a stile at the end of

the field and after a few metres cross another stile and drop down some steps. Turn left and walk along the top of a small ridge for 50 metres. Look out for a stile on your right near a bridge. Cross the stile and turn right onto a road. Retrace your steps to the car park.

TRAIL 18: Haughton Hall - Dukes of Newcastle, 2nd and 3rd Creation

Distance:	14.5 kilometres/9 miles
Start:	Car park on the B6387 in between Bothamsall and Walesby
Maps:	OS Sherwood Forest Explorer 28
	OS Pathfinder 763 (SK67/77) Clumber Park & East Markham
Refreshments:	None
Toilets:	None
Key features:	Sections of the Robin Hood Way, the site of Haughton Hall, the site of Bothamsall's motte and bailey castle and Conjure Alders where the River Maun meets the River Meden

In connection with Welbeck Abbey and Bolsover Castle we met the 1st Duke of Newcastle Upon Tyne, William Cavendish. This dukedom, through a lack of male heirs, became extinct. In the second creation John Holles, whose principal house was **Haughton**, became 1st Duke of Newcastle Upon Tyne. Again, this dukedom became extinct and Thomas Pelham Holles was at a later date granted the Dukedom of Newcastle Upon Tyne in a third creation. Likewise, this dukedom produced no male heir, but on this occasion the 1st Duke was able to engineer a 2nd Duke by obtaining special permission for the dukedom to pass to his nephew.

It was this 2nd Duke who decided to build at Clumber and abandon the Holles' country seat at Haughton Hall. Haughton Hall fell into ruins and now there is nothing left of it.

The site of the motte and bailey castle at Bothamsall

ROUTE INSTRUCTIONS

1.   Follow the clear track out of the back of the car park and under a railway bridge. The path continues in the same direction along a field edge with the River Maun on your left. Turn left over a bridge across the river to join the Robin Hood Way and pass Haughton Hall Farm. *The farm stands on the site of Haughton Hall, with only a few of the original stones being incorporated into the farm. It was the family seat of the Holles family, who were the Earls of Clare and later became the Dukes of Newcastle.* The track passes under the railway again and crosses the River Meden before reaching the B6387.

2.   Cross the road and head up a track to Haughton Park House Farm. Turn right in front of the farm and follow the track as it bends to the left around the farm buildings to a gate. Go through the gate and cross over a track immediately in front of you. *This is West Drayton Avenue, which was the Duke of Newcastle's drive from Clumber to his estate at Haughton and beyond.* Pass Beggars Rest on your right, an old gamekeeper's cottage, and enter Elkesley Wood. Turn left at a T-junction and then follow the blue waymarkers to a footbridge on the edge of the wood. Cross the footbridge over the River Poulter

and continue ahead along a field edge to Brough Lane.

3.   Turn left onto this surfaced track and keep left at a fork. Follow this lane to a sawmill. There is a path down the right-hand boundary of the sawmill to a lane. Follow the lane downhill and as it bends to the right take the track off to the left, which soon passes over the River Poulter by a footbridge at Crookford Ford. The path now continues with conifer trees on your left and an open space dotted with trees on your right. At the end of the open space do not

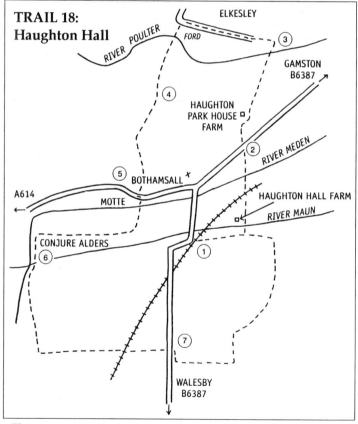

TRAIL 18:
Haughton Hall

ELKESLEY

RIVER POULTER   FORD

③

GAMSTON
B6387

④

HAUGHTON
PARK HOUSE
FARM

②   RIVER MEDEN

⑤ BOTHAMSALL

A614

MOTTE

HAUGHTON HALL FARM

RIVER MAUN

CONJURE ALDERS

⑥

①

⑦

WALESBY
B6387

continue ahead but move over to your right towards a gate. On an electricity pole there is a Robin Hood Way sign pointing the way up a track in between trees to the left of the gate. At the end of the trees the track goes across the middle of a field, following the electricity poles.

4.   At a crossroad of tracks keep ahead to leave the Robin Hood Way. When you reach some buildings on your left, turn left along a field edge by the first building. In the second field you will be walking next to a ditch. When you reach a field corner the path, not visible on the ground, heads across the middle of a field 20 metres to the left of the mound with trees scattered on it in front of you to a signpost by a road. In the summer you may prefer to walk around the field edge. *The mound, Castle Hill, is the site of a medieval motte and bailey castle, which was presumably built to guard the crossing points of the rivers Meden and Maun.*

5.   Turn left into Bothamsall, a Newcastle estate village. After passing the first house on your right, turn right onto a track which doubles back on itself and passes over the River Meden. The track then bends to the right and follows a long clear stretch to join the River Meden. The river forces you to turn left and to reach a historic site of the confluence of the rivers Meden and Maun at Conjure Alders. *Conjure Alders is so named because of its alder trees, which are particularly suited to the surrounding wet conditions.*

6.   Cross a footbridge and turn right. Ignore the second footbridge to rejoin the Robin Hood Way and follow the path into the woods. At a crossroad of tracks keep ahead, passing an open area to your left. The track then continues in between trees on both sides for 100 metres before turning left at a blue waymarker. The path emerges from the trees to follow a field edge. Immediately after passing over a railway the track becomes a path in between a hedge and a fence. Follow this path to the B6387.

7.   Cross over and go into the field opposite. Turn immediately right to follow the field edge and then left at the field corner. At a crossroad of tracks turn left onto a track, which is initially hedged on both sides, and then follows a field edge for 150 metres, before turning sharp right. The field edge leads to Bevercotes Beck. Turn left to walk with the Beck on your right to a stile. Climb the stile and turn left onto a track, which soon bends to the right. After passing

trees on your left Haughton Hall Farm comes into view. At a T-junction turn left and follow the track back to the bridge where you crossed the River Maun. Here retrace your steps back to the car park under the railway bridge.

Clumber Park -
Dukes of Newcastle, 2nd and 3rd Creations

Anyone who has not previously visited Clumber will probably be expecting to see a large magnificent mansion. Indeed, it is a great shame that the house at Clumber no longer stands as in its time it was a truly opulent residence in a memorable setting. However, despite this small disappointment there is plenty to enjoy in this 3,800 acre park, which is managed by the National Trust and is one of Britain's most visited country parks, comprising a mixture of grassland, heath, ancient oak forest and conifer plantation. The focal point of the park is a large lake adorned with a Victorian Gothic Chapel, an elegant classical bridge and a Greek and Roman temple.

Much of the work of the National Trust is directed towards the conservation of the enormous diversity of habitats and species that the park, a large part of which is a designated Site of Special Scientific Interest, is able to support. One of the little known facts about Clumber is that it is rated as amongst the most important sites in Britain for spiders.

The area now known as Clumber, or Clunbre as it was called at the time, was recorded in the Domesday Book of 1086 as being two manor farms tenanted by Roger de Busli. Formerly part of Sherwood Forest, much of the land later passed into the hands of Worksop Priory and Newstead Abbey up until Henry VIII's dissolution of the monasteries in the 1530s.

In 1707 John Holles, 1st Duke of Newcastle of the second creation, was granted a licence to enclose Clumber and create a hunting park for Queen Anne. The Duke was killed in a riding accident in 1711 and his estate passed to his nephew, Thomas Pelham. Thomas Pelham-Holles, a notable political figure, was to become 1st Duke of Newcastle of the third creation. However,

Clumber and its hunting lodge remained undeveloped and, as one visitor commented, it was "a black heath full of rabbits having a narrow river running through it, with a small boggy close or two".

It was not until 1768 that the 2nd Duke of Newcastle, Thomas Pelham-Clinton, having abandoned the old Holles family country seat at Haughton, began transforming the landscape of Clumber from a deer park to a grand country estate with a palatial house built using stone from a quarry on his land at Haughton to the designs of the architect Stephen Wright. A mixture of agriculture and woodland surrounded the mansion and pleasure gardens, which was accessed through a number of elaborate gateways next to lodges.

Many of the Dukes of Newcastle were prominent figures of the day. The 4th Duke was a notable opponent of parliamentary reform and his beliefs led to a mob burning down his empty mansion, Nottingham Castle. The 5th Duke held important political offices, but following much criticism on his efforts as Secretary of War when the Crimean War broke out he retired. It was during his retirement that he planted the famous Lime Tree Avenue or Dukes Drive. This 2 mile long driveway, the ultimate status symbol, has a double row of lime trees on each side.

In 1879, whilst the 7th Duke was in residence, much of the mansion was damaged by fire and had to be rebuilt. The architect, Sir Charles Barry, whose work includes the Houses of Parliament, laid the designs. The 7th Duke was also responsible for the Victorian Gothic chapel, "a cathedral in miniature", which still stands so elegantly beside the lake today.

Clumber was at its heyday in the first two decades of the twentieth century when visits from Royalty and locals abounded. However, it was following the Duke's death in 1928 that the decline of Clumber began until the National Trust purchased the park in 1946 and leased some of the surrounding land to the Forestry Commission.

The estate passed to the 7th Duke's nephew, the Earl of Lincoln, who soon closed the house due to rising costs and taxation. In 1937 he auctioned the house's valuable contents and in 1938 the house was demolished. He had planned to build a new house at Clumber, but the park was requisitioned by the War Department and used as an ammunition store, training area and for trials on new machines of war.

TRAIL 19: Clumber Park

Distance:	7.25 kilometres/4.5 miles
Start:	Car park (indicated by white arrow on the road) between Manton Lodge (near A57) and Truman's Lodge (near the B6034) on the edge of the Clumber Estate
Maps:	OS Sherwood Forest Explorer 28
	OS Pathfinder 763 (SK67/77) Clumber Park & East Markham
Refreshments:	The cafe near the main car park
Toilets:	Near the main car park
Key features:	The Clumber Estate including the chapel, Lime Tree Avenue and lakeside views and a section of the Robin Hood Way

ROUTE INSTRUCTIONS

1.   From the car park cross the lane and head along the signposted public bridleway to join the Robin Hood Way. Ignore all side turnings to reach Clumber Lane. Turn left and continue straight ahead at a crossroad of lanes in 50 metres signposted for the chapel, shop and restaurant. *A left turn would take you onto Lime Tree Avenue, the largest such avenue in Europe, which acted as the main drive into the estate through the elaborate and ornate Apleyhead Gate. In 1906, to prevent the heavy damage being inflicted by insects on the lime trees, bands of black grease were painted around the tree trunks to trap the insects. These bands can still be seen today.*

2.   Follow this lane until it bends to the left to the main car park. On this bend head for the signpost to the shop and restaurant. *The lake and the former site of the house at Clumber are on your right. The 87 acre lake was constructed over fifteen years by the damming of the River Poulter in 1774. In recent years mining subsidence has necessitated extensive work. In 1817 a one-third scale naval frigate, the* Lincoln, *joined the* Salamanca *as a floating summerhouse. On occasions the timbers of the latter, which was accidentally burned in World War II, can be seen in the water near the boat dock.*

3.   Keep the buildings to your left, passing the information point, and make your way to the left-hand side of the chapel. *The Chapel of*

St Mary the Virgin was built between 1886 and 1889 using blocks of locai white Steetley stone and Runcorn sandstone. It has undergone much fairly recent renovation due partly to mining subsidence. In the early twentieth century the 7th Duke used the area in front of the chapel as a golf course. The path bends to the right around the chapel and continues parallel to the lake in between rhododendron bushes through the original pleasure grounds with its Roman Temple. *Glimpses of the Greek Temple can be seen on the other side of the lake.* At a crossroad of paths turn left and in 50 metres reach a metal ornate gate. After 100 metres go through a kissing gate and turn right and follow the lakeside path. Eventually you are able to turn right to cross the lake. In the middle of the lake turn right onto a lane.

4.   As you reach the edge of the lake turn immediately left off the lane, leaving the Robin Hood Way to follow a track with the lake on your left. Ignore all side turnings and essentially keep to the edge of the lake. At the end of the lake turn right at a T-junction. This track

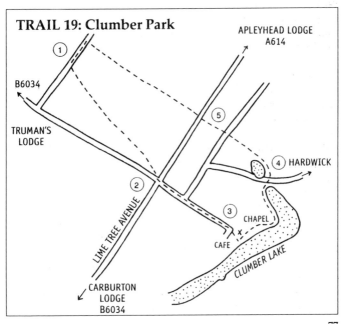

TRAIL 19: Clumber Park

APLEYHEAD LODGE
A614

① B6034

TRUMAN'S LODGE

⑤

④ HARDWICK

②

③

LIME TREE AVENUE

CHAPEL

CAFE

CLUMBER LAKE

CARBURTON LODGE
B6034

on your left and open space on your right crosses Green
ontinues on to join a public bridleway before you reach
Avenue.

5.　　Cross the lane and follow the signposted bridleway. Keep to
the blue waymarker rather than the track 50 metres to your left. Just
before you reach a lane turn left to follow a path that runs parallel
with the lane. This path joins onto the bridleway that you started out
on. Turn right back to the car park.

TRAIL 20: Clumber Park

Distance:	7.25 kilometres/4.5 miles
Start:	Clumber Bridge car park
Maps:	OS Sherwood Forest Explorer 28
	OS Pathfinder 763 (SK67/77) Clumber Park & East Markham
Refreshments:	Clumber Park Hotel
Toilets:	Hardwick village car park
Key features:	The Clumber Estate including Clumber Bridge, Hardwick village and a section of the Robin Hood Way

ROUTE INSTRUCTIONS

1.　　From the car park walk back towards Clumber Bridge. *This
elegant Palladian bridge was designed by Stephen Wright in 1770 and was
built of local limestone.* Take the second lane on your left and turn left
again onto a track in 20 metres known as Beech Drive. Ignore all side
turnings until you reach a T-junction of large tracks (there is a small
path ahead).

2.　　Here turn left to join the Robin Hood Way on Freeboard Lane.
Keep in the same direction ignoring all offshoots almost until you
reach the A614. Fifty metres before you reach the road there is a T-
junction of large tracks by a National Trust sign. Turn left here and
walk to the Drayton Gate with the road on your right. *Drayton Gate
was one of the main entrances to the estate as it marked the beginning of
the drive to the Duke's Haughton estate.* You leave the Robin Hood
Way here.

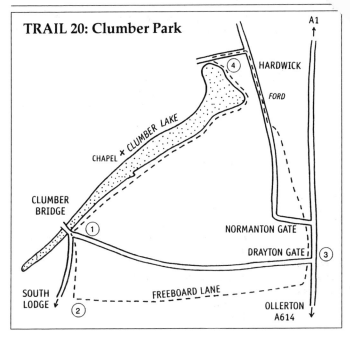

TRAIL 20: Clumber Park

3.   Cross over the lane with the Drayton Gate on your left and follow the path on the other side. This path heads past the gate and then bends to the right. You soon reach the Normanton Gate. *This gateway was built primarily to provide easy access to the Hardwick Estate. Part of the gate was moved to this site from Shireoaks Hall in the nineteenth century. A right turn here would take you to Clumber Park Hotel on the A614.* Cross the lane and pass through a gate. The bridleway heads across fields and emerges out onto a lane just before a ford. Cross the bridge over the ford and pass through Hardwick village. *The village was initially developed by the 5th Duke to provide accommodation for the estate workers.* At the end of the buildings turn left at a T-junction onto a lane.

4.   On reaching Clumber lake turn left to follow the lakeside path back to the car park, passing the Greek Temple along the way. *The area opposite where the house stood was known as the South Lawns.*

TRAIL 21: Clumber Park

Distance:	9.75 kilometres/6 miles
Start:	The main Clumber car park next to the chapel, shop and restaurant
Maps:	OS Sherwood Forest Explorer 28
	OS Pathfinder 763 (SK67/77) Clumber Park & East Markham
Refreshments:	The cafe near the main car park
Toilets:	Near the main car park
Key features:	The Clumber Estate including the chapel, Lime Tree Avenue, lakeside views, Truman's Lodge, Clumber Bridge and a section of the Robin Hood Way

ROUTE INSTRUCTIONS

1.   From the car park turn right following the sign for the shop and restaurant and turn left in 20 metres at another sign. Pass the shop and restaurant on your left and head directly to the edge of the lake. Here turn left to follow a lakeside path across the terraces of the pleasure ground passing several ornate seats. At the end of the path turn left, then immediately right at a fork and right again to reach a gate.

2.   Pass through the gate and cross open ground to another gate in 100 metres. Continue straight ahead, climbing gently uphill. At a clear crossroad of tracks turn left through coniferous woodland. The track leaves the woods and eventually becomes a surfaced lane. A cottage is passed on your right and then a pleasantly situated cricket pitch on your left.

3.   At a T-junction turn right onto the Robin Hood Way. At Clumber Crossroads go straight across (Lime Tree Avenue is on your right) and in 50 metres turn right onto a public bridleway. At a fork keep in the same direction and follow the clear track, ignoring all side turnings as far as a bench 100 metres before a lane. Here turn left onto a clear track, leaving the Robin Hood Way, which meets Clumber Lane. Turn right and walk to the pay point in front of Truman's Lodge.

4.   There is a track on the left opposite the pay point. Follow this

Rufford Abbey (Trail 13)
Rufford Abbey - rear view (Trail 13)

Clumber Lake in Clumber Park (Trail 20)
Lime Tree Avenue, Clumber Park - a double row of trees on each side
(Trail 23)

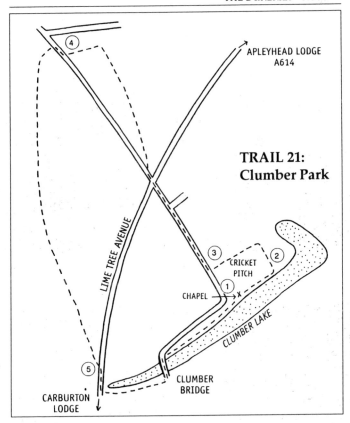

track through Forestry Commission coniferous woodland to a lane.
5.   Turn right and go over Carburton Bridge. After the bridge take
the first left before the lodge (the second left goes over a stile) and
follow the lakeside path to Clumber Bridge. Turn left over the
bridge, stopping to admire the view of the chapel in the distance.
After the bridge turn immediately right to join the path with the lake
on your right. As you get close to your starting point several paths
can be taken back to the car park.

Clumber Park - ornate seat in the pleasure gardens

TRAIL 22: Clumber Park

Distance:	8 kilometres/5 miles
Start:	The Hardwick village car park on the Clumber Estate next to Hardwick Grange Farm
Maps:	OS Sherwood Forest Explorer 28
	OS Pathfinder 763 (SK67/77) Clumber Park & East Markham
Refreshments:	Clumber Park Hotel
Toilets:	Hardwick village car park
Key features:	The Clumber Estate including Hardwick village and a section of the Robin Hood Way

ROUTE INSTRUCTIONS

1.   From the car park walk away from the lake following the Robin Hood Way back on to Hardwick Top Road. Turn right passing Hardwick Grange Farm on your right. A ford and footbridge take you across the River Poulter. After 100 metres take a path in the corner of a field on your left. The path heads diagonally across the field heading for the corner of a plantation and then on to a gate.

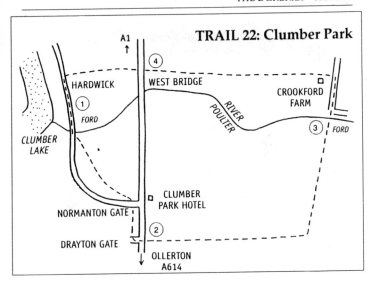

TRAIL 22: Clumber Park

Pass through the gate and cross over the lane at Normanton Gate. Clumber Park Hotel is over to your left on the A614. There is a clear track on the opposite side of the lane, which leads to the Drayton Gate.

2.   Turn left onto the lane and take great care crossing the busy A614. There is a track on the opposite side. Follow this track in the same direction for 1.75 kilometres to a crossroad of tracks at a signpost in open countryside. Turn left here to follow the overhead cables across a field and then into woodland. On reaching an open space head over to the track on the right, which leads to Crookford over the River Poulter. Shortly after the ford you meet a lane at a bend.

3.   Keep straight ahead on the lane leaving the Robin Hood Way. After 100 metres turn left onto a bridleway. This track passes Crookford Farm on your left. Half way along this track you briefly disappear into woodland. On emerging from the trees the track now runs close to the River Poulter on your left to reach the A614 just to the right of the West Bridge.

4.   Again, exercise great care in crossing this main road and head

through the gate on the opposite side. The path winds through woodland to a gate and then follows one side of a plantation. Pass between two fences and then follow the track across the middle of open fields back to Hardwick village. Turn left on reaching Hardwick Top Road. The car park is on your right in 100 metres.

TRAIL 23: Clumber Park

Distance:	8 kilometres/5 miles
Start:	The main Clumber car park next to the chapel, shop and restaurant
Maps:	OS Sherwood Forest Explorer 28
	OS Pathfinder 763 (SK67/77) Clumber Park & East Markham
Refreshments:	The cafe near the main car park
Toilets:	Near the main car park
Key features:	The Clumber Estate including Lime Tree Avenue

ROUTE INSTRUCTIONS

1.   From the main car park turn left onto the lane passing the cycle hire centre on your left. As the lane bends sharply to the left carry on in the same direction. You are soon faced with a choice of routes. Climb the stile in front of you and walk across the middle of a field into woodland. At a T-junction turn left and right after 20 metres. This track runs downhill to the lake. Cross the lake and in the middle turn right onto a lane. Follow Engine Hill to a T-junction.

2.   Walk across the T-junction to join a public footpath through woodland. At a fork keep straight ahead. On reaching a field the School House property can be seen in the middle. Head for a yellow waymarker on the far right-hand side of the property and then follow the fencing around to another waymarker. Here walk 50 metres diagonally across a field to the edge of a plantation and then continue in the same direction to another waymarker. Turn right onto a track for 100 metres. At another waymarker turn left and walk diagonally, initially over rough ground and then across a field to the edge of a plantation. Just inside the woodland turn left onto a track, which leads to Lime Tree Avenue.

TRAIL 23: Clumber Park

APLEYHEAD LODGE

SCHOOL HOUSE

LIME TREE AVENUE

CRICKET PITCH

CARBURTON LODGE

HARDWICK

CLUMBER LAKE

3. Turn left onto Lime Tree Avenue and walk on the right-hand side of the lane in between the double row of trees. At a crossroads continue ahead and look out for a public bridleway signed to the left at the edge of a plantation. Immediately leave the bridleway by forking off on a grassy path to the right, which heads to a corner of trees and then onto Green Lane. Turn right and after 150 metres turn left onto a path which crosses the lane. This path leads to another lane. Turn left towards the lake and after 50 metres, where a track crosses the lane, turn right.

4. At a crossroad of tracks turn right. This path leads out of the woodland and becomes a surfaced lane. Just before the cricket pitch on your left, turn left onto another lane, which soon becomes a rough track and leads you back through trees and then a right-hand bend back to the car park.

The Chesterfield Canal

The Chesterfield Canal was one of the first generation of canals to be built at the beginning of the Industrial Revolution. The construction of the 46 mile length from Chesterfield to West Stockwith, where it joins the Trent, took from 1771 to 1777 under the guidance of James Brindley. The driving forces behind the promotion of the canal included the London Lead Company, which needed a more efficient means of moving lead from its Ashover Smelting Mill, the coal owners of North East Derbyshire, and the Cavendishes who owned the furnaces and forge at Staveley. For its time, it was a superb example of engineering, including the country's largest tunnel at Norwood and one of the earliest staircase locks near Thorpe Salvin.

The canal provided an artery for trade through Derbyshire, Yorkshire and Nottinghamshire, but it remained isolated from the main canal network and the size of boats that could use it was very limited. Coal was the main cargo, but other items such as stone, lead, timber, corn and lime were also carried. Probably the most famous loads were the stone taken from the quarry of the Duke of Leeds near North Anston, which was used to rebuild the Houses of Parliament after a fire in 1834.

However, like most canals the coming of the railways in the mid-nineteenth century signalled the beginning of the canal's decline. To try to minimise the impact, the canal company formed its own railway and canal company. This combined company ultimately became part of the Great Central Railway. An added problem was the Norwood Tunnel, which had always proved difficult and expensive to maintain, and following another collapse in 1907 it was decided not to reopen the tunnel and the Derbyshire end of the canal was cut off.

By the 1950s all commercial trading had ceased, but following extensive campaigning the 26 miles from West Stockwith to Worksop, which is in the hands of British Waterways, was made navigable for pleasure craft. The remaining 20-mile length from Worksop to Chesterfield is currently being restored for full

Chesterfield Canal

navigation of the canal and work is progressing well under the impetus of the Chesterfield Canal Society, which was formed in 1976.

The working boats that once plied the canal were all drawn by horse and were known as Cuckoos, which has led to the towpath being named the Cuckoo Way.

TRAIL 24: Turnerwood and Anston Stones

Distance:	9.75 kilometres/6 miles
Start:	Layby on both sides of A57 by the entrance to Anston Stones Wood
Maps:	OS Pathfinder 744 (SK48/58) Aughton & Carlton in Lindrick
Refreshments:	Public houses in South Anston
Toilets:	None
Key features:	A section of the Cuckoo Way, Turnerwood, Anston Stones Wood and Lindrick Dale

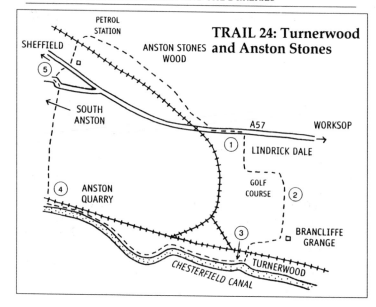

TRAIL 24: Turnerwood and Anston Stones

ROUTE INSTRUCTIONS

1. Facing Worksop on the A57 turn right up Lindrick Dale opposite Lindrick Hill Farm. *A feature of this walk is that the whole area is rich in limestone. On both sides of the lane are exclusive houses and gardens.* At a junction of public footpaths turn left up a track, which soon heads into woodland and follows yellow posts across two of the fairways of Lindrick Golf Club. *Please take care crossing the golf course and respect the players.* At a T-junction of tracks turn right. Pass over a bridge and head uphill.

2. At the top of the hill the path drops gently down out of the woodland and on to Brancliffe Grange. Cross a stile and turn right at a junction of tracks. Cross two further stiles and follow the path with a canal feeder on your left to another stile. Carefully cross the railway line and another stile and continue to keep the feeder on your left. The path leads to the Chesterfield Canal at the picturesque hamlet of Turnerwood. *Turnerwood was built to house the workers of the nearby quarry.*

3.   Turn right onto the Cuckoo Way at Turnerwood Bridge. *The remains of old quarry workings can be seen along this stretch of the canal, which is currently under restoration. The Sheffield to Retford railway line, which you have already crossed, runs parallel to your right. It was the building of this railway which slowly contributed to the demise of the canal. The Thorpe flight of locks is also passed. These locks were regarded in 1773 as a sensational engineering feat, which made them a great tourist attraction. There are fifteen locks in just over half a mile, including two treble and two double lock staircases. At the time of construction it was the steepest flight of locks in Britain.* Pass under three bridges and just in front of the fourth turn right to leave the Cuckoo Way.

4.   Cross the railway line and as you emerge from the trees continue ahead across the middle of a field. The path reaches the houses of South Anston on your left. On reaching a lane turn left and left again at a T-junction. Follow the road as it bends to the right and turn right at a signpost opposite a church onto Lidsters Lane. This leads to the A57.

5.   Cross the A57 with extreme care and take the path ahead to the left of a petrol station. Again cross a railway line and follow the path down some steps and over a footbridge. At a T-junction turn right

Turnerwood

and then bear left at a fork uphill. At a T-junction of gravel paths turn right. A wall soon appears on your right. The path then passes through a gap in this wall and enters Anston Stones Wood. *This 83 acre wood is situated in a craggy limestone gorge, which is rich in wildlife. It has also uncovered, like other limestone gorges in this area, evidence of early man and animals dating back 10,000 years.* Go down two flights of steps and continue along the top of the gorge, ignoring a third flight of steps off to your right. Eventually you emerge from the trees for approximately 100 metres. As you re-enter the woodland turn right after 10 metres and head down some steps to cross Anston Brook by using a footbridge. Take the track to the left, which leads back to the A57.

TRAIL 25: Worksop, Scofton and the Osberton Estate

Distance:	10.5 kilometres/6.5 miles
Start:	Car park on Memorial Avenue next to the tourist information office
Maps:	OS Sherwood Forest Explorer 28
	OS Pathfinder 762 (SK47/57) Staveley & Worksop (South)

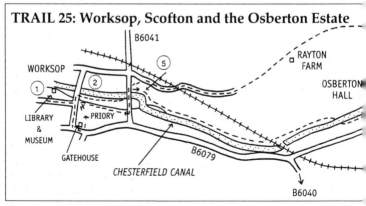

TRAIL 25: Worksop, Scofton and the Osberton Estate

	OS Pathfinder 745 (SK68/78) East Retford (North) & Blyth
Refreshments:	Public houses in Worksop
Toilets:	None
Key features:	A section of the Cuckoo Way, Worksop Priory Church and Gatehouse, Osberton Hall and Scofton Church

The old market town of **Worksop** is known as 'The Gateway to the Dukeries'. The jewel of the town is the ancient Priory Church, which was founded as an Augustine monastery in 1103 by the Lord of the Manor, Sir William de Lovetot. The church is noted for its superb Norman nave and west front, its Early English Lady Chapel and unique well-preserved fourteenth century gatehouse, all of which survived the dissolution. The rest of the church was destroyed and was not restored until the 1920s and 1930s.

Although not actually featured in this walk, as the canal passes through the town centre a warehouse straddles it. This warehouse was the storage depot where the removal firm of Pickfords originated, although it has now been converted into a restaurant on what is known as Cuckoo Wharf.

ROUTE INSTRUCTIONS

1. Facing the car park entrance turn left into the park to walk in front of the tourist information centre/library/museum to emerge onto a road in front of Priory Church. Turn right and then left at the T-junction. The gatehouse is on the corner. Walk around it and back up to the church so that you have completed a small circle. Return to the road and walk over a bridge. Ahead of you is a bridge over the canal. Take the left turn in front of the bridge and turn immediately right to join the canal towpath.

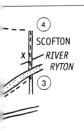

2. Cross over bridge 44 to join the towpath at the other side and walk under the B6041. *Between bridges 44 and 45 the grassed over spoil heap of the former Manton colliery can be seen to the right-hand side.* Pass under bridge 45 and then under a railway viaduct. At bridge 46 go over the bridge and join

the towpath at the other side. *Between bridges 46 and 47 Osberton Hall,
which was the country seat of the Foljambe family, can be seen on the left-
hand side. The 1771 owner had it written into the canal's Act of Parliament
that the towpath must be on the opposite side to the house.* Bridge 48 is
only 100 metres further on. Continue until you reach the next bridge
just after the Osberton lock.

3.   Turn left over the bridge and walk into Scofton, the village of
the Osberton estate, passing a lake on your right which was once a
millpond, and a Victorian postbox on your left. The first signpost off
to the left leads to Scofton church. *The church was built in 1833 by
George Saville Foljambe.* At a junction of public bridleways turn left
onto a wide track.

4.   *On the left are views of Scofton church and Osberton Hall. Evidence
can also be seen of the jumps used in the Osberton cross-country trials.*
After passing Rayton Farm on your left the track becomes a road by
the sewage works. Continue ahead and at a T-junction turn left.

5.   Pass under a bridge and ignore Bracebridge Avenue to your
left. Instead take the next left into Bracebridge. At the B6041 cross
over and walk up the lane over bridge 44 of the Chesterfield Canal.
After passing the next flow of water turn immediately to the right
and follow a path with a hedge on your left. This path returns you
to the road by Priory Church. Retrace your steps to the car park
through the Town Park.

TRAIL 26: Ranby, the Osberton Estate and Scofton

Distance:	12 kilometres/7.5 miles
Start:	Roadside parking close to Ranby village hall. The village hall is signposted from the Chequers Inn
Maps:	OS Pathfinder 745 (SK68/78) East Retford (North) & Blyth
Refreshments:	The Chequers Inn at Ranby
Toilets:	None
Key features:	A section of the Cuckoo Way and the Osberton Estate

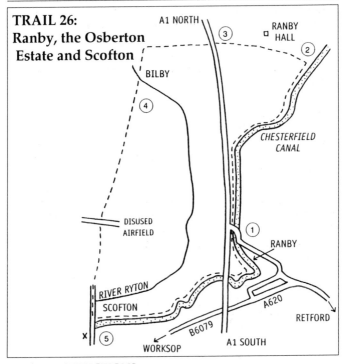

TRAIL 26:
Ranby, the Osberton
Estate and Scofton

ROUTE INSTRUCTIONS

1.   Join the canal towpath by the village hall and turn left. Leave the canal at bridge 52 and turn left to join Green Mile Lane.

2.   *On the right the late eighteenth century Ranby Hall can be seen.* Later you pass some houses on the left and eventually you reach the A1.

3.   With extreme care cross the dual carriageway and turn left down a surfaced lane signposted for Bilby. The lane bends to the left and passes over a bridge across the River Ryton and through Bilby. *There is now nothing left of Bilby Hall, which was long since demolished. The Foljambe family once lived here temporarily whilst their own residence at Osberton Hall was undergoing renovation.* Keep straight ahead through a gate in between two houses. The now rough track crosses

93

open farmland.

4.   At a crossroad of tracks turn left. This track is hedged on both sides and eventually becomes a tarmac lane. Cross the airfield. *This airfield has remained disused since 1960. It became a satellite Bomber Command for RAF Finningley during World War II.* The track continues ahead. *As you approach Scofton evidence can be seen of the jumps used in the Osberton cross-country trials. Scofton is the village of the Osberton Estate. As you walk through it you will pass on your right Scofton church, built in 1833 by George Saville Foljambe, a Victorian postbox, and in the winter views of Osberton Hall, which was the country seat of the Foljambe family. On your left is a lake, which was once a millpond.* Cross the River Ryton and shortly afterwards you reach the Chesterfield Canal. *On your right is the picturesque Osberton lock.*

5.   Your route, however, turns left to rejoin the canal towpath. Pass under bridge 50 and under the A1 to return to Ranby. Leave the canal at bridge 51 to join the road on which you parked.

TRAIL 27: Thorpe Salvin and Thorpe Salvin Hall

Distance:	11.25 kilometres/7 miles
Start:	Roadside parking on Hawthorne Avenue off Sheffield Road in South Anston
Maps:	OS Pathfinder 744 (SK48/58) Aughton and Carlton in Lindrick
Refreshments:	The Parish Oven at Thorpe Salvin and public houses in South Anston
Toilets:	None
Key features:	A section of the Cuckoo Way and Thorpe Salvin Hall

ROUTE INSTRUCTIONS

1.   From Hawthorne Avenue turn left onto Sheffield Road and then right at a signpost opposite a church onto Lidsters Lane. This leads to the A57. Cross the A57 with extreme care and take the path ahead to the left of a petrol station. Cross a railway line and follow the path down some steps and over a footbridge. At a T-junction turn right and then keep in the same direction at the next fork. Pass under a railway bridge and then walk between Anston Brook and

The ruined Thorpe Salvin Hall at Thorpe Salvin

the railway line along the valley bottom of Anston Stones Wood. Ignore all side turnings. Eventually you cross the brook and then pass under another railway bridge before reaching the A57.

2.   Cross the A57 again and turn left. Fifty metres after Lindrick Dale, turn right onto a public footpath. Carefully follow the frequent yellow marker posts onto Lindrick golf course. At a junction watch out for three metal posts on your right. Turn right here to leave the golf course and walk down a track to "The Cottage" on your left. In front of you is a junction of public footpaths. Turn left passing over a river. Ignore the track off to the left and continue with a high hedge on your right under a railway bridge. The track bends to the left and passes several houses. *One has a porch made out of an old rowing boat.* Cross a railway line and then turn right at a public footpath sign in 100 metres. The path goes across a field to a railway line. After navigating the line the path heads for a bridge on the Chesterfield Canal.

3.   Go over the bridge and turn right at the junction in front of you in Old Spring Wood. Follow the waymarkers, keeping the canal on your right to a stile on your right. Climb the stile and walk to another stile on the edge of the wood. On the other side of the stile turn right

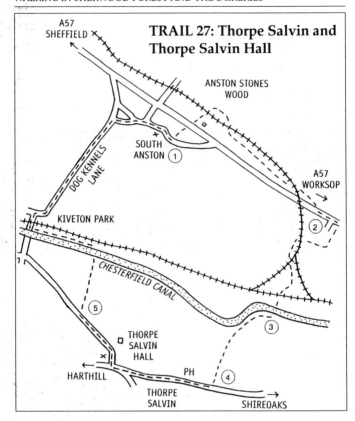

onto a track and bear left at a fork in front of Thorpe Salvin sewage treatment plant. Climb a stile and continue along a field edge, which bends to the right and leads to a lane.

4.   Turn right to walk into the village of Thorpe Salvin, which has a collection of interesting cottages. Take care as the road is not very wide and has no pavement to begin with. Turn right by the church onto Ladyfield Road. On a left-hand bend the ruins of Thorpe Salvin Hall can be seen on your right. *The gatehouse and three-storey entrance facade stand on private land and can only be viewed from the road. The*

The Osberton Lock on the Chesterfield Canal (Trail 25)
The Gatehouse at Worksop (Trail 25)

Spa Ponds (Trail 29)
The Church of St Peter and Paul, Church Warsop (Trail 32)

house was probably built around 1570 and is believed to be a design of Robert Smythson. Follow the road past some houses on your right. Opposite a house on your left there is a bridleway to the right.

5.   This leads down to the Chesterfield Canal where you go over Thorpe Bridge and turn left onto the Cuckoo Way, which you follow to Kiveton. Cross the railway line to leave the canal and turn right onto Dog Kennels Lane. You can walk on the pavement into South Anston. *There are extensive views as you walk along the lane. Kiveton and Todwick can be seen over to the left. In between the two Kiveton Hall, the country seat of the Duke of Leeds, once stood. South Anston is a combination of old cottages and more modern properties.* Turn right by the "No Entry" sign onto High Street. This leads onto Sheffield Road and passes a church, which takes you back to Hawthorne Avenue.

Textiles, Coalmining and the Railways

TRAIL 28: Cuckney

Distance:	12.75 kilometres/8 miles
Start:	Cuckney church/village hall car park, Norton Lane
Maps:	OS Sherwood Forest Explorer 28
	OS Pathfinder 762 (SK47/57) Staveley & Worksop (South)
	OS Pathfinder 779 (SK46/56) Mansfield (North) and part of Sherwood Forest
Refreshments:	Greendale Oak in Cuckney
Toilets:	None
Key features:	Cuckney, a section of the Robin Hood Way and part of the ancient Sherwood Forest

Cuckney is a pleasant and unspoilt Welbeck Estate village on the River Poulter, which once had three mills.

St Mary's Church, Cuckney

The parish church, St Mary's, dates back to Norman times with later extensions. It is a long building with a heavily buttressed tower.

- Close to the church there was probably a twelfth century motte and bailey castle, which it is believed was built by Thomas de Cuckney.
- A mass burial was discovered around the site in the 1950s. Again, the history is a little sketchy, but research suggests it relates to a battle between King Edwin of Northumbria and Pendia of Mercia.
- Also near the church is an old pinfold, where stray animals were once impounded, a fee being payable to the church warden for their return.
- To the west of the church stands Thomas de Cuckney's former manor house.

The school, which now has its top storey removed, was once a mill. It was built in 1723 as a corn mill and was converted to a cotton mill around 1785. The workers were mainly pauper children from London and one of its owners was Hollins, who owned the Pleasley Mills. The mill closed in 1844, but was converted to a school in 1866 by the Duke of Portland. It is still used for the same purpose today.

The Greendale Oak pub is named after a large Sherwood oak, which was situated on the Welbeck Estate. In 1724 the Duke of Portland entered into a wager with the Earl of Oxford that on his estate he had a tree large enough to drive a carriage through. A hole was cut in the tree and the Duke won his wager. Now all that remains of the tree is a stump.

ROUTE INSTRUCTIONS

1. Turn left out of the car park and walk past the church on your left. In 50 metres turn left over a stile by a signpost. Turn left to walk along the top of a ridge for 50 metres. There are some steps on your right followed by two stiles in quick succession. Walk along a field edge with the fence on your right. At the end of the field climb a stile onto a lane.

2. Turn right to join the Robin Hood Way and walk into Norton. At a T-junction turn left and follow the road as it bends to the right.

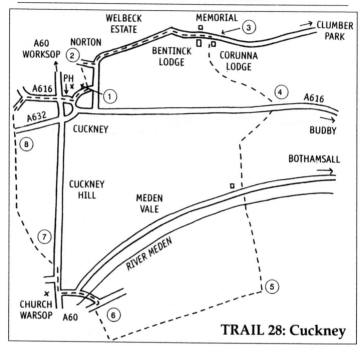

TRAIL 28: Cuckney

Continue past an entrance to the Welbeck Estate near the Great Lake and Carburton Forge Dam. Walk past Bentinck Lodge on your right. *Opposite the lodge is a memorial to Lord George Bentinck, brother of the 5th Duke of Portland, who died whilst out walking close to this spot in 1848. Lord Bentinck was a well-known political figure of his time, who was regarded as a potential Prime Minister. The memorial has a quotation from Disraeli upon it.* At the side of Corunna Lodge turn right onto a track.

3.   Follow the track through woodland to the A616 at Hazel Gap.

4.   Cross the road and follow the track at first with a field on your left and then with woodland on both sides. Before you emerge from the woodland, look out for a signpost and path off to the left. Follow this to a road with Gleadthorpe Lodge on your right. Cross the road and continue ahead on a surfaced track over the Meden. At a

crossroad of tracks turn right to shortly leave the Robin Hood Way.

5.   The path emerges from the trees and continues ahead alongside a field edge with the hedge on your right. At a crossroad of tracks go straight ahead. At a T-junction by the sewage works turn left and follow the path across the middle of a field. At the field edge turn left. At a crossroads turn right and walk under a bridge and on to a road.

6.   Turn right and then immediately left and over the Meden. At a T-junction turn left and right at the next T-junction onto the A60 at Warsop. Pass the church on the left and after 100 metres turn left over a stile by a signpost.

7.   Walk diagonally across two fields. In the third field head for the corner of the woodland. Follow the yellow waymarked path into and through Oakfield Plantation to a stile. Climb the stile and at the T-junction immediately in front of you turn right onto the access road of Park House Farm, which leads to the A632.

8.   Cross the road and climb the steps and stile. The path winds up and over a small hill, which was once the waste from the mill pond, down to Cuckney Dam. Turn right and in 50 metres turn right by the primary school. *In days gone by this was the mill described above.* Turn left at a T-junction and right onto the A616 by Cuckney Village Stores and Tea Room. Cross over at the main road and continue straight ahead. Turn left by the Greendale Oak public house and left again back into the car park.

TRAIL 29: The Maun Valley

Distance:	12.75 kilometres/8 miles
Start:	Maun Valley Trail car park on Old Mill Lane
Maps:	OS Sherwood Forest Explorer 28
	OS Pathfinder 779 (SK46/56) Mansfield (North) and
	part of Sherwood Forest
Refreshments:	None
Toilets:	None
Key features:	A section of the Maun Valley Trail

The River Maun runs through the heart of Mansfield. **Mansfield** was once a small market town in the centre of Sherwood Forest, which was to become a major cotton-spinning town supported by at least ten mills adjacent to the river. From cotton, Mansfield then became a coalmining centre in the nineteenth century.

In 1516 the manor of Mansfield was given to the Duke of Norfolk. From the Norfolks the manor passed to the Shrewsburys, the Newcastles and then to the Portlands.

The centrepiece of Mansfield remains its market place, which has a large unfinished gothic memorial to Lord George Bentinck, son of the 4th Duke of Portland and a great friend of Prime Minister Disraeli, who died in 1848.

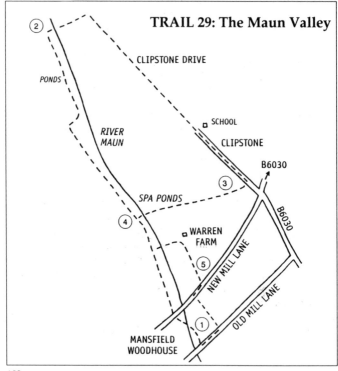

One of Mansfield's most striking structures is its railway viaduct built in the nineteenth century. It has fifteen arches spanning the town centre, making it one of the largest viaducts in an English town.

ROUTE INSTRUCTIONS

1.   Leave the car park through a kissing gate and follow the clear path with the river on your left to a bridge. Go over the bridge and turn right at a T-junction. The path leads to New Mill Lane. Cross over and follow the track ahead. You will pass Warren Farm on your right. At a crossroad of tracks keep ahead. The track eventually bends sharply to the right and then to the left. The next stretch, between the River Maun on your right and a series of ponds on your left, which is frequented by fishermen, is particularly pleasant. Ignore the first bridge off to the right, but cross over the river at the second.

2.   At a junction of tracks take the middle track and then turn right at the next two T-junctions to join Clipstone Drive. This bridleway leads into the housing of Clipstone and at this stage the track becomes a surfaced road.

3.   Before the T-junction with Clipstone Road East, turn right at the signpost for Spa Ponds. *This nature reserve was established in 1984 and is managed by Nottinghamshire Wildlife Trust. It comprises three spring-fed ponds thought to date back to the fourteenth century and a modern pond.* The path leads to the ponds and then crosses the River Maun.

4.   At a crossroad of tracks turn left to retrace your steps in the opposite direction, but only as far as Warren Farm. Turn left towards the farm and cross a stile by the river. Just before the farm buildings there is a stile on your left. Go over this stile and walk with the farm buildings on your right. Go through a gate to join a surfaced track and walk past the front of the farmhouse. This track continues to New Mill Lane.

5.   Turn right, and in 50 metres at a signpost a left turn takes you onto Stinting Lane. On reaching Old Mill Lane turn right back to the car park.

The Pleasley Trails Network and Lady Chatterley's Lover

COALMINING AND THE RAILWAYS

Until the arrival of deep coalmining, which was accompanied by a rapid expansion of the railways for transport purposes, the area's landscape was dominated by the Hardwick Estate. The network, made up of the Teversal, Rowthorne and Meden trails, uses the track beds of the former railways serving Teversal (1868), Pleasley (1871) and Silverhill (1875) collieries, Pleasley Mills and their associated villages.

The heyday for the railway lines was in the early twentieth century, but since the 1930s they gradually declined. Rowthorne was the first to close in 1938 and the final section shut in 1978. There are now no working pits in the area. Since the closures, the lines have been colonised by nature and are now regarded as important corridors of wildlife. Indeed, parts of the trails run through magnesium limestone and are able to support distinctive plant types, which has led to them becoming designated Sites of Special Scientific Interest.

One lasting reminder of the area's industrial heritage is the Pleasley colliery engine house and headstock, which dominates the landscape for miles around. The Friends of Pleasley Pit are currently restoring it.

Pleasley Mills - Pleasley Vale, a steep sided valley on the River Meden, has been the home to mills since the thirteenth century. However, out of the original mills grew a dynasty of textile mills utilising first water power, then steam and finally electricity. Henry Hollins founded the textile mills in the late eighteenth century. From 1846 to the 1980s the mill complex traded as William Hollins Company. It was then taken over by the international Coates Viyella plc, but was finally closed in 1987. The three mills still standing were built in 1847, 1850 and 1913 and have been turned into industrial units.

Lady Chatterley's Lover - D. H. Lawrence (1885-1930), who was born and lived 12 miles from Teversal, set his last and most controversial and shocking novel in the rural Nottinghamshire coalfields. The book was published privately in 1928, but it was not for over thirty years that the complete version was published following an infamous trial which unsuccessfully attempted to ban it on the grounds of obscenity. In the modern day it is now regarded as one of the twentieth century's greatest literary achievements. Many of the important locations can be identified from the book, for example:

- Teversal was referred to as 'Tevershall'
- Teversal Manor was 'Wragby Hall', home of Sir Clifford and Lady Chatterley
- Oliver Mellor's (the gamekeeper) cottage was set at Norwood
- Norwood was where Mellors had his hut of rustic poles
- Hardwick Hall was 'Chadwick Hall'

TRAIL 30: The Pleasley Trails Network and Lady Chatterley's Lover

Distance:	9.75 kilometres/6 miles
Start:	Meden Trail car park on Outgang Lane
Maps:	OS Sherwood Forest Explorer 28
	OS Pathfinder 779 (SK46/56) Mansfield (North) and part of Sherwood Forest
Refreshments:	None
Toilets:	None
Key features:	A section of the Creswell Archaeological Way and a section of the Meden Trail

ROUTE INSTRUCTIONS

1.   Stand in the car park facing the road and take the path from the car park off to the right along the Creswell Archaeological Way. Follow the path through woodland, ignoring all side turns, until you reach a stile. Climb the stile and turn right onto the road. The road bends to the right to enter the Pleasley Mill complex. However, your route takes a left turn at the signpost for the Archaeological Way.

2.   The surfaced track passes an engineering company on your

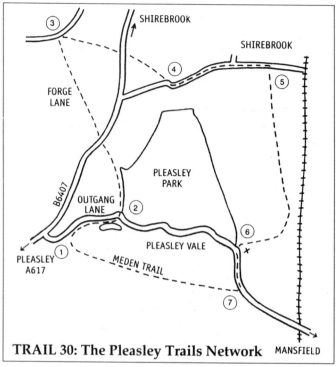

TRAIL 30: The Pleasley Trails Network MANSFIELD

right and then follows the edge of Pleasley Park to reach the B6407. Cross the road and continue ahead on the clear track, Forge Lane, hedged on both sides.

3. Just before you reach a road turn right onto another track hedged on both sides, called Green Lane. Cross the B6407 again and continue ahead to another road.

4. Turn left and follow the road to the edge of the housing at Shirebrook. On reaching the housing continue in the same direction towards Woodland Farm. Just in front of the farm turn right to walk around the edge of a large metal gate on to a track hedged on both sides.

5. Follow the track until you can see a bridge to the left. The track

bends sharply to the left to the bridge. At the bend, climb the stile (wooden barrier and concrete slab) on your right to leave the track and continue ahead along a valley bottom. Climb a stone stile. *Limestone outcrops can be seen.* Cross another stile and shortly afterwards turn left onto a track. Turn right in front of a church onto a lane and continue to a T-junction.

6.   Turn left. *A row of Victorian Cottages can be seen to the right.* Shortly after passing a warehouse on your left, turn right into a small car park for the Meden Trail.

7.   Pick up the trail at the end of the car park. After passing two old railway bridges the trail drops down steeply to a T-junction of tracks in front of the River Meden. Turn right and after 50 metres take the left fork across a footbridge over the river. Ignore the stile immediately off to the left and follow the path back to the car park.

TRAIL 31: The Pleasley Trails Network and Lady Chatterley's Lover

Distance:	11.25 kilometres/7 miles
Start:	Teversal visitor centre, Carnarvon Street, off Fackley Road
Maps:	OS Pathfinder 779 (SK46/56) Mansfield (North) and part of Sherwood Forest
Refreshments:	Visitor centre
Toilets:	Visitor centre
Key features:	Locations used by D.H. Lawrence in *Lady Chatterley's Lover*, Teversal, a section of the Teversal Trail, and the Pleasley Colliery Engine House and Headstocks

ROUTE INSTRUCTIONS

1.   Pass the pit wheels salvaged from one of the local collieries and the displays at the end of the car park and go through a gate. Take the left fork and after 50 metres turn left at a T-junction. Pass under a bridge and continue straight on at a crossroad of paths until you reach a road. Turn right and walk under a bridge. Take the first right onto Buttery Lane. When the lane bends sharply to the left continue straight on through a gate, and into the picturesque village of

Pleasley Colliery Engine House and Headstocks

Teversal, passing St Katherine's Church on your left, and go through another gate onto a lane.

2.   At a T-junction turn left and when you reach the church again, cross a stile to your right into a field. Take the left fork diagonally across the field to a stile. Cross the stile and continue to the far right-hand corner of the field to another stile. Turn right onto a lane. Shortly after passing two cottages on your right there is a stile on the left.

3.   Cross the stile onto a track and pass over a railway bridge. When you reach the end of the hedging on both sides of the track turn immediately right to follow a path across the middle of a field to a lane. Turn left to head towards the houses of Norwood. As you reach the houses look out for a public footpath sign on your right.

4.   Climb the stile and follow the wall to your right. At the end of the wall, walk across the middle of a field into Norwood. Continue in the same direction through the wood to emerge at a footbridge. Cross the middle of a field to a stile. Climb the stile and the next stile a few metres ahead to enter a field.

5.   Continue across the middle of four fields to a lane. Cross the

lane and continue ahead along the edge of two fields with the hedge on your left to another lane. Turn right and when the lane bends sharply to your left continue ahead along the track until you reach a T-junction of tracks.

6.   Turn right onto Longhedge Lane and follow this until you are opposite the Pleasley headstocks on your right. At a crossroad of paths 100 metres after a public bridleway sign turn right onto the Teversal Trail.

7.   After 200 metres cross a lane and continue ahead on the trail

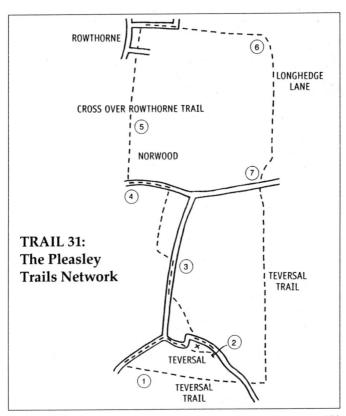

going over a bridge and then under a bridge. Ignore steps off to the right and then at a junction of paths take the right fork. After 20 metres pass through a gate signposted the Teversal visitor centre. Ignore all side turnings until you have gone under a bridge. As a second bridge, which you could walk under, comes into view take the fork off to the left back to the car park.

TRAIL 32: Warsop and The Carrs

Distance:	8 kilometres/5 miles
Start:	Mill Dam car park off the A60 between the Church of St Peter and Paul and the River Meden
Maps:	OS Sherwood Forest Explorer 28
	OS Pathfinder 779 (SK46/56) Mansfield (North) and part of Sherwood Forest
Refreshments:	Public houses in Warsop
Toilets:	None
Key features:	Mill Dam and The Carrs, St Augustine's Church at Sookholme and The Hills and The Holes

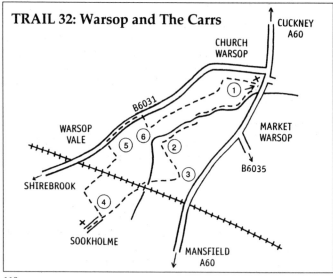

TRAIL 32: Warsop and The Carrs

Warsop is made up of several settlements:

Church Warsop, north of the River Meden, represents the old settlement, although a mining community was added as the pits expanded.

- The church of St Peter and Paul is in a beautiful setting and represents a fine example of church architecture, which was probably built in late Saxon or early Norman times.

- Warsop Old Hall - The Manor of Warsop came into the possession of the Earls of Rutland in 1508. In 1675 it was bought by Sir Ralph Knight and remained in his family until 1846. The last Knight left the manor in his will to Sir Henry Fitzherbert of Tissington. Sir Richard Fitzherbert is still a local landowner.

- The Water Mill for grinding corn was built in 1825. It was seriously damaged by fire in 1922 and restored by 1924.

Between Church Warsop and Market Warsop there is a large open space with the River Meden running through it. This was once marshland and its name, **The Carrs**, comes from the Danish word meaning marshy place. The Carrs are now maintained as a recreational area.

Warsop Vale sits opposite Church Warsop over to the west and was built in 1900 to house the miners at Warsop Main Colliery.

In between Church Warsop and Warsop Vale are the **Hills and Holes**, which are noted for their birds and wild flowers. This is an area of humpy ground created by the shallow quarrying of limestone, some of which was used to restore Southwell Minster after the civil war.

ROUTE INSTRUCTIONS

1. From the car park join the nearest bank of the River Meden and turn right to follow the surfaced path along the riverbank. Cross the second footbridge and continue to follow the path alongside the river.

2. At the third footbridge turn left to leave the river. You soon join a road. Take the first right off this road on to The Hawthorns.

3. At a T-junction turn right onto a dead-end road, which continues as a track. The track crosses the Meden again and then goes under a railway bridge. Continue past Herrings Farm on your right until

you reach the tiny *St Augustine's Church at Sookholme, which has Norman features and dates back to around 1100.*

4.   Retrace your steps to Herrings Farm and turn left onto a path, which is tree lined on both sides. As you emerge from the trees at a junction of paths turn right and walk under the railway bridge. Cross the middle of a field and pass through a gate. After 10 metres turn left to join a track. Follow this to a gate and turn right to reach the B6031.

5.   Cross the road and turn right to walk on the pavement. After 300 metres turn right at a signpost, almost opposite a large red brick house, onto a path which is initially surfaced and hedged on both sides. Just before you reach the river turn left at a junction of paths. After 100 metres pass through a gate and immediately afterwards turn right at a junction of paths.

6.   Cross the middle of the field. In the next field you meet a junction of paths at which you turn left to reach a signpost. Turn right and walk diagonally across the field to reach a sports field. Here, take the surfaced path to your left, which follows the perimeter of the sports field and later bends to the right to return to the car park.

TRAIL 33: Whaley Thorns and Poulter Country Park

Distance:	12.75 kilometres/8 miles
Start:	Poulter Country Park car park on Whaley Lane, virtually opposite Mill Farm
Maps:	OS Sherwood Forest Explorer 28
	OS Pathfinder 779 (SK46/56) Mansfield (North) and part of Sherwood Forest
	OS Pathfinder 762 (SK47/57) Staveley and Worksop (South)
Refreshments:	Public houses in Whaley and the Jug and Glass at Nether Langwith
Toilets:	None
Key features:	Whaley Thorns visitor centre, Poulter Country Park, a section of the Creswell Archaeological Way, the Old Hall at Langwith

Whaley Thorns heritage centre on Cockshutt Lane, Whaley Thorns, is set in a former Edwardian infant school, in what until fairly recently was the heart of the Derbyshire/Nottinghamshire coalfields. This 'hands on' museum provides a fascinating insight and helps to widen the appreciation of the area's heritage using exhibitions from the Stone Age to the coal mining industry of the Victorian period through to their closure. The museum was opened in 1992 by the Creswell Groundwork Trust and is designed to pick up the story told in the displays at the nearby Creswell visitor centre.

In between the heritage centre and Poulter Country Park the Robin Hood railway line will soon run through from Mansfield to Worksop.

The reclaimed Langwith Colliery, which produced coal from 1896 to 1978, has been cleverly landscaped into **Poulter Country Park**. It is owned by Derbyshire County Council and is a quickly maturing mixture of paths, trees and shrubs. From what was once the top of a spoil heap, there is an extensive and very pleasant 360 degree view on a clear day with plenty of seats to enjoy it.

Scarcliffe Park was a gift to Thurgarton Priory by Ralph De Eudo in the twelfth century. After the dissolution it passed into the hands of various landowners including the Duke of Devonshire. Chatsworth Estates now manage it and access is strictly limited to a marked public bridleway.

ROUTE INSTRUCTIONS

1. From the car park turn right onto the road passing Mill Farm on your left. Keep left at a junction and at a signpost in 50 metres on the left join the Creswell Archaeological Way.

2. Turn left in front of Red Brick Cottage. Before you reach Mill Farm the marked path turns to the right to head across a field to Scarcliffe Park. Keep to the marked path through the woodland and at the far end of the trees take the path to the right. This soon bends to the left and follows a path hedged on both sides passing the Old Hall and joining the A632.

3. Turn right and at a pair of cottages, *one of which used to be an inn*, turn left over a stile. *Over to the right is Langwith Bassett Cave. In 1903 the local vicar and his sons discovered early human remains and the bones of animals including arctic fox, woolly rhino and brown bear.* The path

runs down to the valley bottom to cross the River Poulter and then heads back uphill to a stile on the right-hand side of Langwith Bassett church. Continue ahead alongside the churchyard wall to the road. *Langwith is known by the locals as Langwith Bassett, after the Bassett family.* Turn left to leave the Creswell Archaelogical Way and take the next two right turns. The road bends to the left and at a signpost turn left onto a track just before Langwith Bassett primary school.

4.   Cross a bridge over a disused railway and cross another bridge over an operational railway line. Turn immediately right after the bridge to walk along a field edge with the hedge on your right. At a junction of tracks continue ahead through a plantation. When you

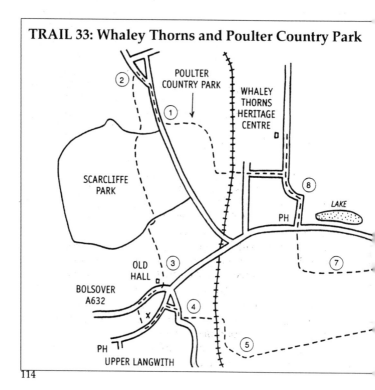

TRAIL 33: Whaley Thorns and Poulter Country Park

emerge from the woodland, continue for 100 metres in the same direction until you reach a disused railway track bed hedged on both sides.

5.   Turn left and follow this for 2 kilometres to a road. *Along the way and over to the right you can see the remains of Warsop Main Colliery beyond Warsop Wood.*

6.   Turn left and after 50 metres turn left into Cuckney Hay Wood at a signpost by a barrier. Continue along the same diagonal path through the wood, ignoring all side turns until you reach a junction which is about 50 metres from the far side of the wood. If you continue ahead here the path drops downhill and out of the wood. Our path turns left and emerges from the wood after 300 metres. At the end of the wood continue in the same direction along a field edge with the hedge on the left.

7.   At the corner of the field turn right and follow the clear path through the trees until you reach a stile in front of Top Farm. Turn right onto a track and follow it downhill and then round to the right. The track emerges on to the A632 just after Brook House Farm. Cross over onto Limes Avenue. *The Jug and Glass public house over to the left by the River Poulter is in a wonderful setting.*

8.   The road bends to the left into Whaley Thorns and then to the right. The Whaley Thorns heritage centre is 150 metres ahead on the left-hand side. Retrace your steps and turn right onto Main Street.

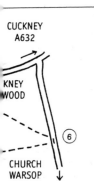

9.   At a roundabout turn left onto Bathhurst Terrace and then immediately right onto a track, which goes over a bridge. The track bears to the left and passes a bench on your right next to a right turn. Continue to the next bench on your left and turn right at a junction of paths. The path heads uphill to a bench and then bends to the left towards four benches in a square at the top of a hill. After pausing to admire the view from the benches, continue in the same direction over the brow of the hill to reach another track in 50 metres. Follow this as it winds back down the hill and turn off to the right to return to the car park.

TRAIL 34: Poulter Country Park, Whaley and Elmton

Distance:	11.25 kilometres/7 miles
Start:	Poulter Country Park car park on Whaley Lane, virtually opposite the remains of an old railway bridge
Maps:	OS Sherwood Forest Explorer 28
	OS Pathfinder 762 (SK47/57) Staveley and Worksop (South)
Refreshments:	Public house at Whaley and Elmton
Toilets:	None
Key features:	The villages of Whaley and Elmton, Poulter Country Park, and a section of the Creswell Archaeological Way

This is probably a walk best saved for a clear winter's day when the hedges have been cut back and the views are extensive. The walk utilises quiet country lanes to view the picturesque cottages of **Whaley** and **Elmton**, which contrast sharply with the old mining community at Whaley Thorns, before entering **Poulter Country Park** for the final leg.

ROUTE INSTRUCTIONS

1.   From the car park walk back towards the road and join a path on your right by a pond. The path runs parallel to a lane along the edge of the park. At a fork keep left to continue in the same direction. When the path begins to bend to the right up a hill keep ahead to a gate 20 metres in front of you. Go through the gate and turn left into another of the Poulter Country Park car parks. Turn right onto the road, passing Mill Farm on your left. At a junction the road bends to the left and passes through the village of Whaley. *Watch out for Forest Cottage on your right and look up the driveway to the side of an old barn, which has an interesting ornamental feature in the wall.*

2.   Turn right at the Black Horse public house. When you reach a T-junction of lanes there is a path on your left up a bank just before the junction, which then follows a field edge initially with a fence,

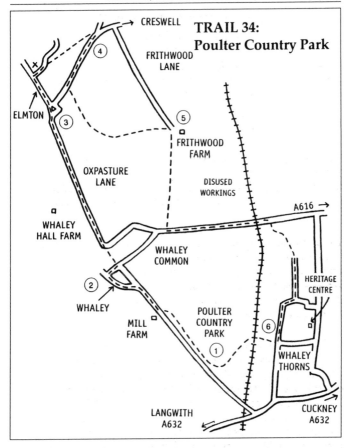

and later a hedge, on your right. At a sharp bend on a lane there is a stile in a stone wall on your right. Climb the stile and turn left onto Oxpasture Lane. You will pass Whaley Hall Farm on your left.

3.   At a triangular junction turn left and immediately left again to walk through the village of Elmton. Turn right onto a lane in front of St Peter's Church. *There has been a church on this site since Saxon*

117

times and it is mentioned in the Domesday Book. The church was largely rebuilt in the eighteenth century to a slightly unusual design. Just before the lane bends to the left leave the lane by a signpost on your right to join the Creswell Archaeological Way and follow a field edge with a wall on your left. At the end of the wall go through a gate and walk across the middle of three fields, crossing two stiles. In the fourth field follow the field edge to a road.

4.   You join the road at a T-junction and turn right. Ignore the first signpost to the left at Green Farm and head for the next signpost 150 metres further on. Follow the field edge with a hedge on your left to a T-junction of tracks. Turn left and then in 20 metres turn right to follow more field edges.

5.   Just before you reach a lane turn right at a signpost onto a wide track hedged on both sides. *The disused workings of the former Creswell pit can be seen on your left.* At a lane turn left. Cross over a railway line carefully and after 50 metres turn right onto a track. Turn left in 10 metres through a gate at a signpost. Pass through another gate and then turn right to walk with the farm buildings on your right. The path leads to a stile in a very poor condition. Climb over it and head for the houses in front of you where you join Moorfield Lane. Follow this road with the former pit terraced houses on both sides to a T-junction and turn right onto The Woodlands.

6.   Turn right onto a tarmaced path at a roundabout, passing a small car park on your left. The path goes over the railway line and bends to the left into Poulter Country Park. The path goes uphill and then back down. At a fork, keep to the left and follow the path around a right-hand bend, which then leads back to the car park.

119

120   PRINTED BY CARNMOR PRINT & DESIGN, PRESTON, U.K.